The
Biscuit Basket
Lady

The Biscuit Basket Lady

*Recipes from
a Vermont Kitchen*

·Mary-Jo Hewitt·

HEARST BOOKS • NEW YORK

Dedicated with love to Clayton and Jackie,
the two most important people in my life

•

Copyright © 1995 by Mary-Jo Hewitt

It is the policy of William Morrow and Company, Inc., and its imprints and affiliates, recognizing the importance of preserving what has been written, to print the books we publish on acid-free paper, and we exert our best efforts to that end.

Library of Congress Cataloging-in-Publication Data
Hewitt, Mary-Jo.
The biscuit basket lady : recipes from a Vermont kitchen / Mary-Jo Hewitt.
p.   cm.
Includes index.
ISBN 0-688-13269-3
1. Biscuits.   2. Muffins.   3. Cookery—Vermont.   4. Basket making.
I. Title.
TX770.B55H48   1995
641.8′15—dc20   94-17025
                                                    CIP
Printed in the United States of America

First Edition

1 2 3 4 5 6 7 8 9 10

BOOK DESIGN BY JESSICA SHATAN
ILLUSTRATIONS BY JOHN T. BURGOYNE

·Contents·

·How the Biscuit Basket
Lady Came to Be·

I made my first cake at the age of eight, in bed, during one of many recurring bouts of rheumatic fever. My mother, who was a great cook, was also an inventive woman. Knowing I had to be kept relatively quiet, she started teaching me to cook. She placed the necessary ingredients for a cake on a large wooden bread board, and brought them into my room. She explained and carefully oversaw what needed to be done, then carried the batter-filled pan to the oven. After the cake had finished baking and cooling, she brought it back to me for frosting.

Most women of my generation learned to cook from their mothers—usually not in bed, but at a fairly young age. As we grew older, we relied on Fanny Farmer's *Boston Cooking School Cook Book* or Irma Rombauer's *Joy of Cooking* for instructions on how to do what our mothers left out.

But then sometime in the sixties homemaking became almost taboo, and the kitchen was not the place mothers chose to entertain their children. While women raised their consciousness cooking took a back seat. Many of the young people growing up in this era never learned how to cook.

For people of this generation, who I hope will benefit most from this book, my message is this: Cooking is fun, not a challenge. Everything you cook needn't be company fare. Don't be intimidated. You're in your own kitchen. Since you may not have a lot of time to experiment, I offer these more or less foolproof recipes.

Look somewhere else for precise instructions on how to select fish, roast meat, or prepare and cook vegetables. Here, I teach you to cook down-to-earth dishes you can always fall back on. Pretend you're spending an hour or so in my Vermont kitchen every time you open this book. As you read a recipe, I hope you'll feel as if you're standing by my work table, watching me. I've spent a lot of years doing just that with young friends. So now I'd like *you* to join me in my kitchen while we make the simple things that make mealtimes at home more fun than eating out.

You'll find detailed instructions for some dishes, while other recipes will give you opportunity to experiment. Every once in a while you'll find me saying "never, never, never" do such-and-such, and there'll be a good reason for it. But most of the time, it's your kitchen and you're in charge. You'll find out soon enough when a recipe needs to be followed exactly. And you'll also discover that you have more ingenuity than you thought you had.

Ingenuity. Now there's a wonderful word. One of its synonyms is *invention*, and one of my mother's favorite sayings was "Necessity is the mother of invention." As if to prove her right, almost everything I've done in my lifetime has come about as the result of necessity. You might say I've invented myself as I've gone along.

Until my children were almost grown I did what most women of my generation did: I stayed home and kept house. Naturally this included a good deal of cooking and baking, which meant collecting lots of recipes along the way. Never one to throw away anything that might prove useful some day, I kept them.

Once the children no longer needed my nurturing, I decided to finish my college education. At the age of fifty-one I became a teacher. But as I'm fond of saying, "I went into teaching late in life and got out early." What I'd pinned my dreams on turned into a nightmare. After three years I quit and wondered what to do with the rest of my life.

Previous summers I earned a little pin money baking biscuits during strawberry season for the Morse Farm. When I found myself with no classes to prepare and no children underfoot, I was able to expand my repertoire and bake for Morse's all summer.

This was also the summer I was introduced to basket making. My friend Kathy Dutil had just learned to make a basket and decided to share her knowledge with me. Halfway through the lesson I was hooked.

That fall and winter I read all I could about basket making, and took every lesson offered. By spring I'd made over a hundred baskets, and even though I'd given away many of them, I still had a large inventory. Our local farmers' market seemed like the perfect place to sell baskets as well as baked goods.

You must understand that at a farmers' market no one is recognized by his or her given name. There's the Egg Lady, the Honey Man, the Goat Milk Lady, and so on. Biscuits were my most popular baked item, so soon I was known as the Biscuit Lady. Since I also sold baskets, there were those who called me the Basket Lady. When jokingly pressed to identify myself as one or the other, I had to admit that I wasn't sure if I was a biscuit-baking basket maker or a basket-making biscuit baker. That's how the Biscuit Basket Lady was born.

When *Yankee* magazine featured me as a Great New England Cook, they needed eight recipes to go with the article "In Search of the Perfect Biscuit." That trove of old recipes I'd been keeping finally found a purpose. I hadn't looked at most of them in years, and they recalled many fond memories of times and friends almost forgotten. Reminiscing was fun, but I feared I'd never figure out the scribbled versions of some of those old recipes.

Since the things I make now are either in my head or in the small current file on my counter, I toyed with the idea of discarding most of the old recipes. Fortunately, before I did I was approached about writing this cookbook.

But cooking is only one side of my life. The other side is devoted to baskets. Making baskets and teaching others to make them have become passions. While baking for the farmers' market occupies my summer, basketry takes up my winters. I never tire of either.

I'll never forget the first time I served homemade bread in a handmade basket. (Strange isn't it that we speak of "homemade" food, but "handmade" baskets?) It gave me the kind of satisfaction I could never describe. In the hope that you might enjoy the same pleasure, some basket "recipes" are also included in these pages.

If you've never made a basket, before you attempt one please consult the basic basketry book suggested in the Mail Order Sources (page 200). Just as the cooking recipes assume you know how to beat the eggs, stir in the flour, or boil the broth, the basket recipes assume you know how to recognize the right and wrong side of reed, the difference between spokes and weavers, and how to lash a rim.

I hope this book will satisfy your urge to cook and kindle an interest in basketry, as well. May its pages have many drip marks, grease-stained fingerprints, and carefully penciled notations.

The
Biscuit Basket
Lady

Doing It My Way

L ike everyone else, I have definite ideas about a well-equipped kitchen. Although I do a lot of production baking, my kitchen equipment is basic, so you needn't feel intimidated. My biscuits are baked one sheet at a time in an ordinary noncommercial oven. Here is what you'll need to follow the recipes in this book.

Probably the most important piece of equipment in my kitchen is my heavy-duty *food mixer*. Mine happens to be a KitchenAid, but there are many other good ones on the market. With all its attachments, there's hardly a job my mixer can't tackle. I use it to slice, grate, grind, as well as all manner of mixing chores. A good, heavy-duty food mixer is a useful addition to any kitchen.

Since I can't puree with my mixer, I have a *blender*. Creamed soups would be difficult to perfect without it. It comes in handy for many different tasks—making cracker crumbs, chipping ice, making milkshakes, to name but a few. If you don't own a blender, consider getting one. They're relatively inexpensive.

The following list covers everything else you'll need for the baking recipes in this book:

5 loaf pans 9½ x 5 ½ x 3 inches
1 loaf pan 8½ x 4½ x 2½ inches
One 8-inch square baking pan
1 jelly-roll pan, 10½ x 15½ x 1 inch
1 rectangular cake pan, 13 x 9 x 2 inches
One 10-inch Bundt pan
1 rectangular nonstick griddle (electric or not)
At least 2 aluminum cookie sheets (which can be kept shiny)
At least 2 cooling racks
At least 1 set of measuring cups and spoons
At least 1 spatula and 1 whisk

When folks see the number of measuring cups, spoons, spatulas and whisks on my work table, their first question is always, "Why so many?" Ergonomically and economically, it makes sense to use a fresh utensil every time, put the used one in the sink, and save time, energy, water, and detergent by washing them all at once.

You'll need several sizes of *wire whisks*, and a couple of sturdy *spoons*. Eventually you'll have one spoon that is your favorite. I'm not sure where my pet spoon came from, but I think it was designed to get ice cream out of round commercial cardboard containers. It has a wooden handle, a stainless-steel shaft, and a shallow, slightly rounded work surface ending at a flat edge. Its shape is similar to a curved rubber spatula, but it's much more rugged. Because of its wide work surface (about 2½ inches) and flat bottom, large amounts of batter can be mixed more thoroughly and quickly than with a standard mixing spoon.

A good wooden *bread board* is essential. It's used for kneading dough, rolling out biscuits, and forming loaves. I found that most bread boards were too small, so I designed one to fit my needs. It's made of ⅛-inch-thick birch measuring twenty-five inches square. The board fits into a groove cut halfway through molding. The upper half of the molding makes a lip to keep flour on the board while the lower lip keeps the board firmly secured to the work surface (see Mail Order Sources, page 200).

You'll want a good, sturdy rolling pin. I have a heavyweight marble one. Its weight takes the effort out of rolling, and since marble stays cold, it doesn't heat up doughs containing shortening.

Bowls. Glass and ceramic break, plastic tends to discolor and sometimes retains taste and odor, so stainless-steel bowls are the practical choice. They don't chip or break and can take a lot of abuse. You'll need at least four: small, medium, large, and very large.

You also will want *saucepans* that are small, medium, large, and very large. Heavy is best, and if they match, I say "Hurrah for you."

(I have never owned matching pans and envy anyone who does.) Be sure that your large pot is very heavy because this is the one you'll use for making jams, pickles, soups, and some casseroles. A Dutch oven that will hold five to six quarts is perfect for these jobs. Your largest pot—the one you'll use for canning—should hold eight to ten quarts. Stainless-steel is best. Mine is aluminum and, for this reason, needs constant scouring.

And speaking of scouring, choose *cookie sheets* that can be kept shiny top *and* bottom. This guarantees that cookies, rolls, and biscuits won't be overbrowned or tough on the bottom. Trust me on this.

Get a *scale* and learn to weigh. Although not absolutely necessary, a kitchen scale *is* handy. Once you get into the habit of weighing dough rather than gauging it by eye, you'll be pleased at how uniform your finished products are. Loaves that weight the same, bake the same. This is also true for dinner rolls and bread sticks. Since the dough rises as you are looking at it, you can't trust your eye for size when it comes to yeast items.

Another reason to use a scale is that a scooped cup of flour can weigh as much as six ounces when it should weigh only four. In a recipe calling for four cups of flour, you could conceivably add a cup and a half more than needed, ruining a recipe. Get a scale and learn to weigh!

And now let's talk about *towels*. I was lucky enough to inherit some fine old linen tea towels from my husband's aunt. I use them all the time to cover rising dough, to line bread baskets, and of course to roll jelly-roll cakes. A couple of cotton towels (not terry cloth) will serve the same purpose, but linen is *so* nice. I've seen linen towels advertised in cooking catalogues. Get hold of some. It will take a few launderings to soften them up properly, but they last and last and last.

Some wise person once said, "To be happy, surround yourself with things you love." With this in mind, I have one last suggestion for a well-equipped kitchen: surround yourself with things you love—art, plants, flowers, children, good friends, happy memories.

Biscuits
Plain and Fancy

It took me almost thirty years to come up with a biscuit recipe that really pleased me, and my Basic Biscuits (page 11) is it. For years I've been selling these biscuits at the Capital City Farmers' Market and several shops in Montpelier. Folks love them. The best compliment, though, came from a six-year-old boy whose parents had been buying my biscuits at one of the shops in town. At my farmers' market stand he recognized them immediately and called his father over to buy some. While waiting, he looked up at me with awe on his face (something I'd never seen before, or since) and asked, "Are *you* Mary-Jo?" When I told him I was, he said, almost breathlessly, "You make the best biscuits in the world."

Needless to say, this child became one of my favorite people. Less than a year later he spent some time in my kitchen learning how to make them himself. If a seven-year-old can duplicate my biscuits, it will be a cinch for you.

Not everyone has the same tastes, (thank Heaven!) and after a while I started getting requests for whole wheat biscuits, and then for cheesy ones. It didn't take long to include them in my inventory. My Basic Biscuits are still the all-time favorite, but I hope you'll try all three.

Just remember, the less you fuss with biscuits, the better they are. The more often you make them, the easier it gets.

1. *Be sure your baking sheets are shiny. Otherwise your biscuits will have overbrowned, tough bottoms.*
2. *The dough should feel like Play-Doh, the stuff kids love to play with.*
3. *It is critical the you knead no more than fifteen times. Otherwise you'll get tough biscuits. I urge you to resist the temptation for just one more. It will lead to five more, then ten more. Remember, the magic number to knead is fifteen times.*
4. *I use my thumb joint for measuring how thick to roll out the dough. Almost everyone's thumb joint measures one inch, hence the expression "rule of thumb."*

If you'd like to make a bunch of biscuit batches at one time—after all, you have all the ingredients at hand—buy some dry milk if you don't already keep it in the house. Add $2/3$ cups dry milk to the other dry ingredients, and when you're ready to bake up a batch, simply add ice cold water instead of milk.

The following method for making multiple batches of biscuit mix will save you time and cut down on confusion. On your work surface, lay out the desired number of containers. Measure out your ingredients in the following order:

6 cups (1½ pounds) unbleached all-purpose flour
⅔ cup dry milk
Heaping ½ cup sugar
Heaping ¼ cup baking powder
½ tablespoon salt

(The order of the ingredients has nothing to do with graduated amounts. It has to do with how well one ingredient shows up when poured on top of another. If you're adding salt to ten individual containers of ingredients and are interrupted, you'd have a hard time remembering which batches had gotten the salt if it went on top of the sugar. By adding ingredients in the above order, each is easily discernible from that which preceded it.)

When making multiple batches, read the amount of each ingredient *once* before pouring that amount into each container, read the amount of the next ingredient, add it to each container and so forth until all ingredients have been added in the right amounts to each container. Once all the dry ingredients are measured, add 1 cup (2 sticks) margarine to each.

At this point you can proceed in one of two ways: empty the contents of one container into a large mixing bowl and with a pastry blender, work the margarine into the dry ingredients until it's the right texture; or simply empty the contents of a container into the bowl of your electric mixer, insert the wire whip attachment, cover with a towel (flour will fly), and mix on high speed for 15 seconds. Once this is done, pour the mixture into a plastic bag, twist-tie the top, and put it in the freezer until you need it.

Ergonomically, this system is efficient. When preparing for a church supper, a large party, or like me, a farmers' market sale, the time saved makes a huge difference. And you'll appreciate having mix on hand when you need hot biscuits to transform a humdrum meal into something special.

· Basic Biscuits ·

These biscuits are a delight at any meal, or as a snack with a bit of butter or jam. They're perfect for shortcake, topped with fruit and a dollop of whipped cream. But the very best way to enjoy them is buttered, with a drizzle of warm maple syrup. This makes a lovely little dessert when you haven't planned anything else.

6 cups (1½ pounds) unbleached
  all-purpose flour
Heaping ½ cup sugar
Heaping ¼ cup baking powder

½ tablespoon salt
1 cup (2 sticks) margarine
2 cups cold milk

Preheat oven to 425°F.

Measure the flour, sugar, baking powder, and salt into a large bowl.

With a pastry blender cut in the margarine until the mixture looks like a blend of cornmeal and small peas.

Add the cold milk, and with a large spoon or your hands, mix the dough until it holds together. If some crumbs refuse to join the rest, add a smitch more milk. If the mixture seems a bit soft, add a tablespoon or so more flour.

continued

Place the dough on a floured surface. *Knead no more than 15 times,* then roll the dough out to a thickness of 1 inch. Cut out the biscuits with a sharp 2½-inch round cutter.

Place the biscuits on an *ungreased* baking sheet not touching. Bake for 15 minutes or until golden brown.

Slide the biscuits on to racks to cool. If you intend to serve them immediately, place them in a cloth-lined basket and cover with another cloth.

• Whole Wheat Biscuits •

Makes 24 biscuits

To make these biscuits follow the recipe for basic biscuits, but use 8 cups of the following whole wheat flour mixture, and decrease the milk to 1¾ cups. Other directions remain the same. These biscuits are far more dense than the basic ones and do not rise as high; however, they're my second-most popular item at the farmers' market.

Besides being good at breakfast, they make an ideal accompaniment to soup.

1 part whole wheat flour
1 part cracked wheat (available at
food co-ops and most health food
stores, made from whole wheat
berries)

2 parts unbleached all-purpose flour

•Cheese Biscuits•

Makes 8 to 10 biscuits

This is a nice biscuit to make as a change. The cheddar cheese adds a delightful rich flavor to the biscuits but limits their use slightly. (You certainly wouldn't want to use them for strawberry shortcake.)

2¼ cups unbleached all-purpose flour

1 tablespoon baking powder

⅓ cup sugar

1 teaspoon salt

1 cup grated cheddar cheese

⅔ cup milk

1 egg, beaten

Preheat the oven to 450°F.

Place the flour, baking powder, sugar, and salt in a bowl and, using a pastry blender, work in the cheese until it looks like cornmeal. Stir in the milk and beaten egg, then bring the mixture together into a cohesive mass, adding more flour if necessary to hold the dough together. Knead the dough lightly, about 10 to 15 times.

Place the dough on a floured board and roll it out 1 inch thick. Cut the biscuits with a sharp 2½-inch biscuit cutter and place them on a shiny sheet, not touching. Bake about 15 minutes, until they're golden brown.

Slide biscuits on to racks to cool or place in a cloth-lined basket for immediate serving.

The Biscuit Basket

· The Biscuit Basket ·

This is the first basket I teach to new students. It's the perfect size for holding biscuits, muffins, or sliced bread. If you follow the directions carefully the basket will have a perfect shaker cat-head bottom. (Note: Kits are available for making this basket; see Mail Order Sources, page 200.)

Tools

sharp scissors

tape measure

clothespins or spring clips

a 3- to 5-gallon dishpan or your
   kitchen sink

pencil

awl

Materials

From ½-inch flat reed, 14 spokes
   20 inches long

¼ pound ¼-inch flat oval reed

Approximately 6 feet ½-inch flat
   oval (for rims)

Approximately 3 feet sea grass
   (for filler)

Finished basket measures 7 by 7 inches and is 5 inches high.

Preparation: Soak the spokes for at least 5 minutes in warm water before using. With a pencil, number the spokes 1 through 14 on the wrong side. Mark the middle of spokes 1 and 2 on the wrong side.

The Base: Place spoke 1 vertically on the work surface. Place spoke 2 on top of it, horizontally, forming a cross.

Place spoke 3 vertically, to the east of spoke 1 and overlapping spoke 2.

Place spoke 4 vertically, to the west of spoke 1 and overlapping spoke 2.

Working to the north of spoke 1, weave in spokes 5, 6, and 7.

Working to the south of spoke 1, weave in spokes 8, 9, and 10.

Working to the east, weave in spokes 11 and 12.

Finally, working to the west, weave in spokes 13 and 14.

Take a moment to be sure that your spoke ends line up evenly and that the base measures approximately 5½ inches square. The spaces between spokes should be about ¼ inch wide. (When it's time to weave the sides, always be sure to put one coiled weaver in warm water whenever you take one out.)

Creating the Sides: With the base flat on your work surface, you will work 2 rows from the inside and a third row from the outside. Then, with the sides bent up, all rows are worked from the outside. With the wrong side facing you, place the end of a soaked ¼-inch flat oval weaver on top of spoke 13 with the tip of the weaver lining up with the left-hand side of the spoke. Going from left to right, weave under spoke 4, over spoke 1, under spoke 3, and over spoke 11.

At the corners, bend up spokes 12 and 7 so that they are perpendicular to the work surface. Weave behind spoke 12, and in front of spoke 7. Spoke 12 will remain upright, while spoke 7 will flop down.

Weave to the next corner. Bend up spokes 10 and 12. Weave in front of spoke 10 and behind spoke 12. Spoke 12 will remain upright and 10 will flop down.

On the third corner, spoke 14 will remain up while spoke 10 goes down, and on the fourth corner, spoke 14 will once more remain up while spoke 7 goes down.

To end this row, and all rows that follow, overlap the weaver for 4 spokes and cut it.

Give the base one turn clockwise. Start weaving over spoke 9. When you weave this row, you will be holding up the corner spokes not held up previously.

Flip the base over and make sure that all spokes are flat. Observe the tiny "feet" at each corner. This is the beginning of the cat-head shape.

With the right side of the weaver facing you, start weaving on the opposite side of the base, starting this time on the other end of spoke 9.

When you reach the corner, hold it up from the working surface, but have your spokes pointing downward and close to each other. The remainder of the base stays flat on the work surface. Keep the weaver taut while you weave around the 2 corner spokes. Keep the other spokes flat on the work surface as you weave them. Only the corners come up.

Bend up the sides of the basket at the edge of the base. Do not weave tightly for the next 3 rows. You want the basket to bow out a bit. Continue weaving until the basket is 5 or 6 inches high (less, if you like).

Finishing Up: Cut off the inner spokes flush with the top of the basket. Cut the outer spokes long enough to tuck into at least 2 rows of weaving.

Soak the remaining spoke ends and tuck.

Rims: From ½-inch flat oval, cut 2 pieces the circumference of the basket, plus enough for about 4 inches of overlap. The inner rim should be about 2 inches shorter than the outer rim.

Both rims should overlap in the same area but not on top of one another. After clipping on rims, insert sea grass as filler.

Lashing: Using ¼-inch flat oval, begin lashing just beyond the rim overlaps. This way they are the last parts to be lashed and any slack or tautness is easier to correct. Lash in whatever manner you've found comfortable.

Mastering Muffins

In most basic cookbooks you'll find illustrations of good and bad muffins, as well as instructions about how to avoid the latter. Despite the way commercial muffins look, with their mountain-peak tops, they are *not* what one sees illustrated as good muffins. Those muffins are filled with air holes caused by overbeating. The secret to really good muffins, with a "hill" for a top, is in *not* beating them. One simply uses a spoon to work the moist ingredients into the dry ones. It may take you several attempts to get the desired results, but your perseverance will pay off.

Whenever a muffin recipe calls for baking powder, I use Rumford because it has no alum, an ingredient which adds a slightly bitter taste to the finished product. If Rumford isn't available in your area, look for another baking powder without alum.

The recipes that follow yield twenty-four muffins. My philosophy is if you're doing something once, you might as well save yourself time by making more than you need. Put extras in your freezer for those busy times when fresh baked is not a possibility, or share the fruit of your efforts with someone who doesn't bake.

If your oven doesn't accommodate two 12-cup muffin tins, side by side, halve the recipe. Do *not* attempt to bake two muffin tins on separate shelves. Muffins in the lower tin get overdone on the bottom and underdone on top.

The directions tell you to grease your tins generously, but instead you can use muffin tins that are Teflon coated or paper lined. I've used all three and can't say that I have a real preference. Paper lining the tins guarantees that the muffins will be intact when you remove them from the pan. Accidents do happen occasionally with Teflon-coated or well-greased tins.

Most of the recipes are fairly basic. The fun comes when you start to experiment. Do you like nuts? Almost any muffin recipe can use a few, even if they're not called for. Raisins? Why not? Add a few and see how it goes. The only thing that limits how much you can alter basic muffin recipes is your imagination.

And while we're on the subject of experimenting, be sure to check out the chapter on quick breads (page 111). In it I suggest converting some of those recipes into muffins, so be sure to give them a try.

· Basic Bran Muffins ·

Makes 24 two-inch muffins

Almost everyone has his or her own favorite bran muffin recipe. This is mine. It's quick and easy to make, and the resulting muffins go with almost anything.

3 cups bran cereal
2½ cups unbleached all-purpose
    flour
1 cup sugar
2 tablespoons baking powder

1 teaspoon salt
2 eggs
⅔ cup corn oil
2½ cups milk

Preheat the oven to 400°F. and grease two 12-cup muffin tins.

Stir the dry ingredients together and make a well in them. Combine the egg, oil, and milk and pour this mixture into the well. Stir the mixture gently until no more flour is visible. Fill the prepared tins two-thirds full and bake for 25 minutes or until a toothpick inserted in the middle comes out clean.

Place the muffins on racks for cooling, or into a cloth-lined basket if you'll be serving them soon.

• Blueberry Muffins •

Makes 24 two-inch muffins

When I summered in Maine, my Aunt Tillie made these muffins from berries my cousins and I picked in her woods. She would serve them with soup for supper—a real treat, since they always seemed more like cupcakes than muffins.

5¼ cups unbleached all-purpose flour

1 cup sugar

1 rounded teaspoon salt

3 tablespoons baking powder

3 cups fresh or frozen blueberries (tiny ones are best)

1 cup corn oil

1½ cups milk

3 eggs, well beaten

Preheat the oven to 400°F. and generously grease two 12-cup muffin tins.

In a bowl, stir the flour, sugar, salt, baking powder, and blueberries just enough to mix.

Make a well in the middle of these ingredients and add the oil, milk, and beaten eggs. Stir gently until no more flour is visible.

Fill the prepared tins two-thirds full and bake 25 minutes or until a toothpick inserted in the middle comes out clean.

Place the muffins on racks for cooling, or into a cloth-lined basket if you'll be serving them soon.

•Blueberry Bran Muffins•

Makes 24 two-inch muffins

These are fun to serve on birthday mornings or for weekend guests.

3 eggs
1 cup firmly packed light brown
   sugar
½ cup corn oil
2 cups plain yogurt
1 teaspoon vanilla extract
1 cup wheat germ

1 cup oat bran
2 cups unbleached all-purpose flour
2 teaspoons baking powder
2 teaspoons baking soda
1 teaspoon salt
1½ cups fresh or frozen blueberries

Preheat the oven to 425°F. and grease two 12-inch muffin tins.

Beat the eggs and brown sugar together until well blended, then gently blend in the oil, yogurt, and vanilla. Stir in the wheat germ and oat bran.

Combine the flour, baking powder, baking soda, and salt. Stir the blueberries into the flour mixture. Add the blueberry and flour mixture to the egg mixture and stir gently until no more flour is visible.

Fill prepared tins two-thirds full and bake about 25 minutes or until a toothpick inserted in the center of a muffin comes out clean.

Place the muffins on racks for cooling, or into a cloth-lined basket if you'll be serving them soon.

• Banana Bran Muffins •

Makes 24 two-inch muffins

If you don't have enough ripe bananas, fill the measure with apple-sauce or mashed, canned pears. These are hearty breakfast muffins.

2 eggs

1½ cups packed brown sugar

2 cups mashed very ripe bananas

1 cup raisins

⅔ cup corn oil

2 teaspoons almond extract

1½ cups whole wheat flour

1½ cups unbleached all-purpose
 flour

1 cup oat bran

1 teaspoon baking soda

1 heaping tablespoon baking powder

1 teaspoon ground cinnamon

Preheat the oven to 375°F. and generously grease two 12-cup muffin tins.

Beat the eggs and brown sugar together in a small bowl until well blended. Stir in the bananas, raisins, oil, and almond extract.

Combine the flours, oat bran, baking soda, baking powder, and cinnamon in a large bowl. Add the egg and banana mixture and stir just enough to moisten the dry ingredients.

Fill the greased muffin tins three-fourths full and bake for 20 to 25 minutes or until a toothpick inserted in the middle comes out clean.

Place the muffins on racks for cooling, or into a cloth-lined basket if you'll be serving them soon.

•Peach Muffins•

Makes 24 two-inch muffins

Before individually quick-frozen peaches were available, I made these muffins only during the short season of fresh peaches. Now they can be enjoyed year-round.

4 cups unbleached all-purpose flour

1⅓ cups sugar

2 tablespoons baking powder

1 teaspoon salt

1 teaspoon ground cinnamon

½ teaspoon grated nutmeg

1½ cups milk

½ cup corn oil

2 eggs

2 cups chopped peaches (fresh or
    frozen)

Preheat the oven to 350°F. and grease two 12-cup muffin tins.

Into a large bowl, sift together the flour, sugar, baking powder, salt, cinnamon, and nutmeg. Make a well in these ingredients. Add the milk, oil, and eggs and stir everything together gently, just to moisten the flour. Gently stir in the chopped peaches.

Fill the prepared tins two-thirds full and bake about 25 minutes or until a toothpick inserted in the middle of a muffin comes out clean.

Place the muffins on racks for cooling, or into a cloth-lined basket if you'll be serving them soon.

•Oat Bran Good-for-You Muffins•

Makes 24 two-inch muffins

These muffins are popular not only with the old hippies who frequent the Montpelier Farmers' Market but with folks of any generation who are interested in eating wholesome food that's designed to nourish, do no harm, and taste good. The surprise ingredient in these muffins is tofu. My masseuse suggested using it in place of eggs. I was a bit hesitant, but found it worked very well, and eliminated a good deal of cholesterol. Two muffins and a fruit for breakfast will hold you until noon. (And you'll feel virtuous all morning.)

2 cups oat bran
2 cups raisins
2 cups boiling water
½ cup maple syrup or honey
½ cup corn oil
½ pound firm tofu

4 cups whole wheat flour mix
  (page 12)
2½ teaspoons baking powder
2½ tablespoons baking soda
½ tablespoon salt (optional)
2 cups plain yogurt

Put the oat bran and raisins into a large bowl, pour the boiling water over it, stir to mix, and let it sit for 10 minutes. Meanwhile, grease two 12-cup muffin tins and preheat the oven to 375°F.

Beat the maple syrup, oil, and tofu into the oat bran and raisin mixture and continue beating until everything is well mixed.

Sift together the flour mix, baking powder, baking soda, and salt. Add them alternately with the yogurt to the oat bran mixture, and even though this contradicts what I told you in the introduction to this chapter, *beat well after each addition*.

Fill the muffin tins using a heaping ¼ cup measure for each muffin. The batter should be heaping in the muffin cups. This is not ordinary, but it works for this recipe.

Bake for 30 minutes or until muffins are browned on top. Allow the muffins to cool in the pans for about 10 minutes before moving them to racks for cooling.

• Soy Ploy Muffins •

Makes 24 two-inch muffins

The soy flour in these light, moist muffins contributes an interesting nutlike flavor as well as added protein. Serve them as a dessert with clotted cream and dots of jam, or make them using the following "ploy": Liven them up by filling the tins one-third full of batter, adding a teaspoon of your favorite jam, and filling the tins two-thirds full of batter.

1 cup soy flour

3 cups unbleached all-purpose flour

2 tablespoons baking powder

2 teaspoons salt

4 tablespoons sugar

1 cup raisins

2 eggs, beaten

6 tablespoons corn oil

2 cups milk

Preheat the oven to 425°F. and generously grease two 12-cup muffin tins.

Stir the flours, baking powder, salt, sugar, and raisins just to mix and make a well in these ingredients. Combine the eggs, oil, and milk and pour them into the well. Stir everything together gently just to moisten the flour.

Fill the prepared tins two-thirds full and bake 12 to 15 minutes or until a toothpick inserted in the middle comes out clean. (These muffins do not get brown. They hardly change color.)

Place the muffins on racks for cooling, or into a cloth-lined basket if you'll be serving them soon.

Taking the Terror Out of Yeast Baking

Somewhere along the way a mystique has evolved around the use of yeast. You've probably been told to always "proof" the yeast first, to use water of a precise temperature to dissolve the yeast, and to keep rising dough out of drafts. The list goes on. Working with yeast, I've gotten away with a lot of outrageous antics along the way—all of which proved educational. I'd like to share some of that knowledge with you.

When I was a child, my mother and grandmother used nothing but cake yeast, which is tricky to work with. Perhaps that's where all the rules came from. Today we have instant, granular yeast, which is far less finicky. I buy my yeast in bulk because it's more convenient. Most health food stores or food co-ops carry baking yeast by the ounce or in one-pound portions. Don't be afraid of buying too much yeast at one time. You might be afraid to use an outdated yeast envelope, but be courageous. If you've kept the yeast in the refrigerator—or better yet, the freezer—it will remain active and usable for at least two years. I bought a thirty-pound bag of yeast, kept it in an airtight container in my freezer, and after two years when the bag was empty the last dregs were just as good as the first tablespoons.

Most yeast recipes tell you to "proof" the yeast. That is, you put the desired amount of yeast in lukewarm water with a bit of sugar and wait for it to "look alive," to rise up and bubble a bit. Not necessary! When I make my cinnamon-raisin English muffins, I put warm (not tepid) water in a large bowl, add the sugar, yeast, salt, cinnamon and raisins in no particular order, add the flour, and whip it with a wire whisk. The whole process takes a minute and a half. There's no proofing, and I have never yet experienced a failure.

When I shared this with a chef friend of mine he was, to say the least, shocked.

"But you can't add salt right along with yeast" was his horrified response.

"I do it all the time," I nonchalantly replied.

I'm not sure if he's adopted my method to save time, but I hope you'll try it some time.

And this is probably as good a place as any to share a true tale of what I did once with yeast dough, more from frugality than derring-do. There was a time in my life when I made raised rolls almost every day for a local outlet. I put the dough to rise in the refrigerator before I went to bed, set my alarm for some time in the middle of the night, got up, and punched it down. One night when I sleepily opened the fridge, the dough had not risen at all. Mentally I reviewed that evening's process and felt sure I'd forgotten to add the yeast. No way would those ingredients go to waste. Butter, eggs, sugar, milk—all cost too much!

I placed the dough on my work table, covered it and went back to bed. In the morning when the dough had reached room temperature, I dissolved the proper amount of yeast in more warm water than the recipe called for. I pushed the dough out flat, spread it with the dissolved yeast and rekneaded the whole thing. Finally, I put it to rise. If it didn't do anything, I'd have wasted twenty minutes of time and a little yeast, but if I succeeded I'd saved everything including a good deal of pride. It worked. Those rolls were every bit as good as any made in the conventional manner.

In the yeast recipes that follow, I tell you to dissolve the yeast in warm water before you proceed with the rest of the recipe. That seems like a contradiction of what I've just told you, but it's really a matter of my not pushing *your* luck. I do a lot of production baking, so every few seconds saved adds up, and time is money. When you make only a batch of bread a week, the time it takes to proof the yeast is of no consequence. It is, however, iron-clad insurance that you won't run into any problem with it.

And have you ever wondered what is meant by "knead until dough is smooth and elastic"? My mother, a great bread baker, learned this from her Mom. After about five minutes of earnest kneading (or up to eight minutes of gentler massaging), pick up the mass of dough and bend it downward slightly. If you see little flat bubbles just below the satiny looking surface, your dough is now "smooth and elastic."

For explicit directions about kneading dough, shaping loaves, and baking bread, you simply can't beat those given in *The Joy of Cooking*. If you don't have a copy of this fine basic cookbook, go to your local library and peruse its pages. The information is invaluable.

Let me tell you a little about the workings of a *sponge*. In the recipes for English muffins, I describe the sponge as soft, almost watery. It takes about an hour to rise, then falls back on itself. If you have children around during this process, have them keep an eye on the sponge near the end of an hour. I used to tell my kids that there were little men under the dough trying to get out. They knew I was kidding, but loved to watch the volcanolike eruptions that go on for about ten minutes before the dough collapses. Once the fun is over, the sponge is ready for the second part of the recipe, which includes the addition of oil, more flour, and vigorous mixing.

Make bread once a week. Kneading dough is good for your frame of mind. It gets rid of aggressions and it's much more therapeutic than punching a pillow. I'm firmly convinced that yesterday's homemakers had better mental health than today's because they kneaded dough on a regular basis.

If fear of using yeast has you in its grip, relax. There's almost no way you can kill yeast. And there are so many ways you can use it. Be brave. Experiment. The worst you can do is come up with a brand-new process or an exciting new recipe.

• Basic English Muffins •

Makes approximately 10 muffins

It's an insult to put these fine English Muffins into a toaster. The bottoms and tops are cooked, so the middles need toasting and this is best done under a broiler. I prefer to butter them before broiling, but try it both ways to determine your preference.

1 tablespoon active dry yeast
1½ cups warm water
1 tablespoon sugar
¾ teaspoon salt

¼ cup dry milk
4 cups (1 pound) unbleached
   all-purpose flour
3 tablespoons corn oil

Lightly grease a baking sheet.

In a large bowl, mix the yeast, water, sugar, salt, dry milk, and 2 cups of the flour. This will make a "sponge," which is a soft, almost watery dough. Set it aside to rise for about 1 hour or until the sponge falls back on itself. Add the corn oil, whisk it around a bit, and beat in the remaining flour to make a soft dough that can just barely be handled.

Flour your hands. Lift up and cut off about 4 ounces of dough. (I weigh each one, but by eyeball it looks about the size of a jelly donut.) With your hands still well floured, form a small patty (much as you would do if you were forming a meat patty or tofuburger). Each one should be about ½ inch thick and 3 inches or so in diameter. Place each formed muffin on the greased baking sheet to rise for 30 minutes.

Meanwhile, preheat a nonstick griddle. (If you have an electric griddle, set it to about 325°F. You'll soon see whether 300° or closer to 350°F. works better for your particular griddle.) Lacking a nonstick griddle, use a very large frying pan or an iron griddle that fits over your stove burners and lightly grease. Set heat for medium high. With a metal spatula, lift the raised muffin dough onto the griddle. The muffins need to cook about 6 minutes on each side to be done properly in the middle. If in doubt about their doneness, gently press your finger against the side of the muffin. If the dough feels "done," it is. Trust yourself. You'll know.

When thoroughly cooled, take 2 forks, back to back, and split the muffins through the middle (between the top and bottom). If you choose to freeze some, it's wise to place a doubled piece of waxed paper between the two layers of muffin. This makes them easier to separate when you take them out of the freezer. You can then butter them frozen and immediately pop them under a broiler.

NOTE: If unexpected company drops by, try this easy supper dish. Broil the muffins on one piece of foil while heating rings of pineapple on another. Layer the broiled muffins with cheese, a circle of heated pineapple and more cheese. Return them to the broiler until the cheese melts. Watch them carefully so as not to burn the cheese. It only takes a minute or so. For guests who don't care for cheese, try peanut butter. It combines well with pineapple. If you use peanut butter, do not return them to the broiler.

You can also serve English muffins as mini-pizzas. Broil the muffins and have ready either pizza sauce or drained, canned tomatoes plus your favorite toppings. Place some cheese on a muffin half (I'm partial to cheddar), add the pizza sauce or tomatoes, a little oregano and basil for an Italian touch, and sprinkle on more cheese. Broil until the cheese is melted and the tomato or pizza sauce is heated through.

• Whole Wheat English Muffins •

Makes approximately 10 muffins

These English muffins are much more dense than the basic ones and are very good with soup and for sandwiches.

You can make these muffins in precisely the same manner as the Basic English Muffins (page 33) except for the flour. Before proceeding, make up some whole wheat flour mix (page 12).

•Cinnamon-Raisin English Muffins•

Makes approximately 10 muffins

Once you assemble the ingredients, make these muffins in the same manner as the Basic English Muffins (page 33).

1 tablespoon active dry yeast
1½ cups warm water
1 tablespoon sugar
1 teaspoon salt
¼ cup dry milk
½ cup raisins

½ tablespoon ground cinnamon
½ cup oat bran (optional)
4 cups unbleached all-purpose flour
 (1 pound)
3 tablespoons corn oil

In a fairly large bowl, mix the yeast, water, sugar, salt, dry milk, raisins, cinnamon, oat bran (if you're using it), and 2 cups of the flour. This will make a "sponge," which is a soft, almost watery dough. Set it to rise. See Basic English Muffins (page 33) for further directions.

• Breadsticks •

Makes approximately 18 sticks

A little time-consuming, but lots of fun to make and even more fun to serve, these breadsticks are definitely worth the effort.

1½ tablespoons active dry yeast	½ tablespoon salt
1 cup warm water	1½ tablespoons sugar
3 tablespoons corn oil	3 cups unbleached all-purpose flour
3 tablespoons olive oil	1 egg, beaten

In a large, warmed bowl, dissolve the yeast in the warm water. Stir in the oils, salt, and sugar. Beat in 1½ cups of the flour, and continue beating until smooth. Gradually mix in about 1½ cups more flour to make a stiff dough.

Place the dough on a floured surface and knead for about 5 minutes, until it is smooth and elastic (see chapter introduction). Place in a greased bowl, turning to grease all surfaces. Cover the dough loosely with a cloth towel or plastic wrap and let it rise until doubled in bulk, which should take about 1 hour.

While the dough is rising, grease 2 baking sheets.

Punch the dough down, and measure out ½ ounce dough balls. Lacking a scale, divide the dough into 18 equal portions, each about the size of a walnut. Roll the dough between your palms to form sticks, 10 to 12 inches long and about ¼ inch in diameter. Place the sticks on a greased baking sheet, leaving 1 inch between each. Brush with beaten egg. Let rise for 30 minutes.

About 20 minutes into the rising time, preheat the oven to 350°F. Bake breadsticks about 25 minutes or until golden. Remove to racks to cool.

Depending on the company, serve these in an oversized beer mug or an attractive vase.

•Portuguese Sweet Bread•

Makes 2 loaves

This is a very sweet bread, hence its name. It will go well with almost any meal and is excellent for sandwiches.

2 tablespoons active dry yeast

¼ cup warm water

1 cup sugar

6 cups unbleached all-purpose flour

1 teaspoon salt

1 cup lukewarm milk

3 eggs, beaten, plus 1 egg for
  brushing tops of loaves

Dissolve the yeast in the water and set aside.

In a deep bowl, mix the sugar, 4 cups of the flour, and the salt.

Make a well in the center of the flour mixture and pour in the milk, beaten eggs, and dissolved yeast. Beat this mixture well. Beat in the remaining 2 cups of flour, 1/4 cup at a time, until beating is not possible, at which point resort to your hands or a large sturdy spoon.

Knead for 8 to 10 minutes, until it is smooth and elastic (see chapter introduction). Place in a greased bowl, turning to grease all surfaces. Cover it loosely with a cloth towel or plastic wrap and let it rise until doubled in bulk, which should take about 1 hour.

Grease two 9 x 5 x 3-inch loaf pans.

Punch down the dough and divide it in half. If you've never formed loaves before, or if you have trouble forming loaves, you'd do well to let the dough rest for about 10 minutes. This rest period makes the dough more pliable and easier to handle. If you're short on time you can skip this step. Once the loaves are in the pan, let them rise for 40 minutes. It is not necessary for these loaves to double in bulk before baking them.

About 10 minutes before the loaves are ready for baking, preheat the oven to 350°F. Just before popping them into the oven, brush the top of the loaves with the beaten egg. Bake for 1 hour or until well browned and they begin to come away from the sides of the pan.

Remove the loaves from the pans and cool on racks.

•Swedish Rye Bread•

Makes 2 loaves

A friend once wrote asking me for my recipe for "that wonderful sweetish rye bread." This *is* sweeter than most rye breads, but "sweetish" is not its name.

2 cups water
½ cup brown sugar
1 teaspoon salt
1 teaspoon caraway seeds
1 teaspoon aniseeds
1 tablespoon active dry yeast

3½ cups unbleached all-purpose flour
2 cups sifted rye flour
Melted butter or margarine for tops (optional)

Combine the water, brown sugar, salt, and seeds in a small saucepan and bring to a boil. Continue to boil for 3 minutes. Pour into large bowl and cool to lukewarm.

Place cooled mixture in a large bowl. Add the yeast and stir in the all-purpose flour to make a soft dough.

Add the rye flour to make a stiff dough. Let rise for 1½ hours. Punch down. Turn out onto a floured surface and knead lightly for about 5 minutes. Place the dough in a greased bowl, turning once to grease all surfaces. Let rise until doubled in bulk, about 1 hour.

While the dough is rising, grease two 9 x 5 x 3-inch loaf pans.

When the dough has risen, punch it down and knead again for about 2 minutes. Divide the dough into 2 portions, cover it with a cloth, and let it rest for 5 minutes. (This makes forming the loaves easier.) Place the formed loaves in the prepared pans and let them rise until doubled in bulk (about 1 hour).

Ten minutes before the loaves are ready for baking, preheat the oven to 375°F. Bake the loaves for 45 minutes, until they're golden brown. Remove to racks for cooling. For soft crusts, brush the loaf tops with butter or margarine immediately after taking them out of the pans.

• Herb Bread •

Makes 3 loaves

This recipe originated on the island of Nantucket. It came to me by way of my good friend, Jackie La Bella. She picked it up there, along with the skill to make lightship baskets, for which the island is famous. The original recipe called for honey, but being a Vermonter with easy access to maple syrup, I use that instead. Feel free to use whichever is more available in your area, but keep in mind that almost anything is improved by the use of maple syrup.

Before starting the recipe, I strongly suggest you measure all the herbs in a small bowl. This takes a while, so if it's not done ahead of time one of two things could happen: your water and yeast will have cooled down considerably, slowing the rising process of the bread; or you may discover, having already set the yeast to working and your taste buds to watering, you lack one or more of the herbs.

2½ cups warm water

2 tablespoons active dry yeast

2 tablespoons maple syrup (Vermont Grade B)

2 tablespoons light molasses

2 tablespoons corn oil

1 tablespoon dried rosemary

2 tablespoons chopped dried parsley

1 tablespoon ground dried thyme

½ tablespoon dried basil

½ tablespoon dried oregano

½ tablespoon salt

Few grindings of black pepper

7½ cups unbleached all-purpose flour

Melted butter or margarine for tops (optional)

In a mixing bowl, combine the warm water and yeast. Add the maple syrup, molasses, corn oil, herbs, salt, and pepper.

Add 4 cups of flour, and with a large wire whisk, beat for 2 minutes. (Note: The wire whisk used for scrambling eggs will not handle this job. If you don't have a large whisk, beat the batter with a large, sturdy spoon, lifting it very high, making large circles to incorporate as much air as possible.) Gradually add about 3½ cups more flour, working it in with a spoon or your hands. By the time the flour has been incorporated, you will have a cohesive mass. Pick it up with floured hands and put it onto a floured board. Knead the dough for 8 to 10 minutes, until it is smooth and elastic (see chapter introduction). Place in a greased bowl, turning to grease all surfaces. Cover it loosely with a cloth towel or plastic wrap, and let it rise until doubled in bulk, about 1 hour.

While the dough is rising, grease three 9 x 5 x 3-inch loaf pans.

Punch down the dough and divide it into 3 equal portions. Shape them into loaves and place each in a greased loaf pan to rise until doubled in size. (Note: My handwritten recipe says "let rise to half the original size." Maybe one can achieve that on Nantucket but I wouldn't try for it on the mainland.)

Ten minutes before baking, preheat the oven to 350°F.

Bake for about 1 hour, or until nicely browned and the loaves begin to come away from the sides of the pan.

Turn the loaves onto racks for cooling. For softer crusts, brush the loaf tops with butter or margarine as soon as they are on the racks. Wait until almost cool to cut or you'll run into trouble.

• Charlie's Pride Bread •

Makes 5 large loaves

Don't attempt to halve this recipe; you'll end up with not enough dough for three loaves and too much for two. This bread freezes so well, you'll be happy you have the extra loaves on hand.

continued

2 tablespoons active dry yeast

½ cup warm water

4 eggs, beaten, at room temperature

4 cups warm milk

1 cup corn oil

2 tablespoons salt

¾ cup sugar

1⅓ cups soy flour

1 cup wheat germ

12 cups unbleached all-purpose
flour, plus more for kneading

Melted butter for tops (optional)

In a large, warmed bowl, dissolve the yeast in the warm water. Add the eggs, milk, oil, salt, and sugar and beat slightly. Combine the soy flour, wheat germ, and all-purpose flour in a bowl and stir half of it into the yeast mixture. Beat well for 2 minutes.

Mix in as much more of the remaining flour mixture as needed to make a stiff dough. Knead vigorously for 5 to 8 minutes, until smooth and elastic. Place in a greased bowl and turn to grease all surfaces. Let the dough rise for about 1½ hours, until doubled in bulk.

While the dough is rising, grease five 9 x 5 x 3-inch loaf pans.

Once the dough has doubled in bulk, turn it out onto a floured board and divide it into 5 portions. Form loaves and place them in the prepared pans to rise until doubled, about 1 hour.

Once doubled, place the loaves in a cold oven and set the temperature at 400°F. After 15 minutes, turn the oven down to 350° and bake 30 minutes longer. After 20 to 25 minutes, if you notice the tops are already brown enough, place a sheet of aluminum foil loosely over the loaves.

Remove the loaves from their pans to racks for cooling. If soft crusts are desired, brush the tops of the loaves with butter.

·Hearty Carrot Bread·

Makes 5 loaves

This is the perfect bread to serve with homemade soup on a cold, damp, or snowy evening. Because it freezes so well, you'll be glad you made a lot.

2 cups grated carrots
1 cup yellow cornmeal
1 cup molasses
½ cup honey
1 cup corn oil
½ tablespoon salt
1 tablespoon ground cinnamon

1 cup plain yogurt
2 tablespoons active dry yeast
9 cups whole wheat flour mix
  (see page 12)
Melted margarine for tops
  (optional)

Cook the carrots in enough water to cover them until tender, about 10 minutes. Drain, save the liquid, and add enough more water to make 3 cups liquid. Place in a large bowl. Return the carrots to this liquid and add the cornmeal, molasses, honey, oil, salt, cinnamon, and yogurt. Stir it around a bit and let it cool to lukewarm.

Add the yeast and 5 cups of the flour mix. Stir until you have a cohesive mass, then let it sit for 10 minutes. Add anywhere from 3 to 4 cups more flour mix until the dough is heavy enough to knead.

continued

Knead for 8 to 10 minutes, until dough is smooth and elastic (see chapter introduction). Place in a greased bowl, turning to grease all surfaces. Cover loosely with a kitchen towel and let it rise until doubled in bulk, about 1 hour.

During this time grease five 9 x 5 x 3-inch loaf pans.

If you're in the middle of other things, punch it down once more and let it rise again. The more this bread gets punched down, the finer the texture of the finished product. When ready, punch down and place the dough on a floured surface. Divide into 5 equal portions. Form loaves and place in prepared pans. Let rise for 1 hour or until doubled in bulk.

During the last 10 minutes of rising, preheat the oven to 350°F.

Bake the loaves for about 1 hour. Check in 45 minutes to see that the loaves are not getting too brown. If so, cover them loosely with aluminum foil. When the loaves come away from the sides of the pans and have a hollow sound when you knock on them, they're done.

Remove them from the pans to racks for cooling. If you prefer soft crusts, coat the tops lightly with margarine once loaves are out of the pans.

•Dinner Rolls•

Makes about 30 two-ounce rolls

When the occasion calls for something more formal than biscuits, these dinner rolls are perfect. They freeze well, but if you don't have time to form thirty rolls, halve the recipe.

1 tablespoon active dry yeast
¼ cup warm water
2 eggs, well beaten
1¾ cups warm milk
½ cup corn oil
½ cup sugar

1½ tablespoons salt
6 cups unbleached all-purpose flour
1 egg, beaten with 2 tablespoons
*   milk, or 2 tablespoons melted*
*   margarine, for brushing tops*

Combine the yeast and warm water in a large bowl. Add the beaten eggs, milk, oil, sugar, and salt. Mix well. Stir in 3 cups of the flour and beat for 2 minutes. Gradually stir in the remaining flour as needed to produce a dough that is no longer sticky. You should be able to just barely pick up the mass with floured hands. (Note: Your rolls will pick up more flour in the kneading process. Do not add too much flour now, or the result will be tough rolls.)

On a floured surface, knead the dough for 5 to 8 minutes, until smooth and elastic (see chapter introduction). Place the dough in a greased bowl, turning to grease all surfaces. Cover it loosely with a towel or plastic wrap and let it rise until doubled in bulk, about 1 hour.

Punch down the dough and place it onto a floured board. If you don't have a scale to measure the dough in 2-ounce pieces, divide it into halves, then quarters. Divide each quarter into 7 to 8 equal pieces. You should have about 30 pieces.

To make pretty little knot shapes, form a 6-inch "snake" by rolling the dough between the palms of your hands. Holding one end of the snake in each hand, curl 3 inches of the center in a circle, with about 1½ inches free at each end. Tuck the top end under and into the circle, and tuck the other protruding end over and into the circle. This takes practice, but the results are worth it. Place the rolls on a greased, shiny baking sheet about 3 inches apart. (An easier but not so fancy method is to form a smooth, flat roll by patting the dough between the palms of your hands or to make ladyfinger shapes.) Brush the rolls with either the egg and milk mixture, which will make them slightly crisp and brown, or the melted margarine, for softer, more tender tops. Let the rolls rise until doubled in bulk, about 45 minutes.

Preheat the oven to 425°F.

Bake the rolls for 8 to 10 minutes, depending on your oven. Check at 7 minutes to see how they are doing; they should be nicely browned and feel "done" when touched on the side. Immediately put them on a rack to cool, or into a cloth-lined basket if you'll be serving them soon.

· Bagels ·

Makes 32 bagels

These bagels go well with any soup; topped with jam, toasted or plain, they make good breakfast fare; and they can't be beat for sandwich making.

2 tablespoons active dry yeast
2 cups warm potato water (see Note)
4 eggs, beaten, plus 2 egg yolks,
   beaten with 2 tablespoons water
1 tablespoon salt

1 tablespoon sugar
¼ cup corn oil
8 cups unbleached all-purpose flour
10 quarts water mixed with ¾ cup
   sugar

continued

Soften the yeast in the potato water. Add the beaten eggs, salt, sugar, oil, and 2 cups of the flour. With a wire whisk, beat this mixture for 2 minutes. Gradually stir in the additional flour to achieve a stiff dough.

Before you start kneading and shaping, bring the 10 quarts of water and sugar to a boil in a large kettle. Preheat the oven to 425°F. and grease 2 cookie sheets.

Knead the dough for 2 to 3 minutes and let rise till double—about 40 minutes. Divide into 32 equal portions, and form the bagels. Measure out 3 ounces of dough (the size of a small tangerine), and either roll into a sausage about ¾ inch in diameter by 6 inches long, wet the ends, and seal, or roll the dough around in your hands to form a ball, push your index finger through the middle, then twirl it a few times to enlarge the hole. The latter method is more fun; the former method is more foolproof.

After 5 or 6 bagels are formed, let them rest for 20 minutes, then place them into the boiling sugared water and boil for 3 minutes, turning them over once. They will first sink to the bottom and then rise to the top.

Remove the bagels from the water with a slotted spoon, allowing any excess water to drip off. Carefully place each bagel on a greased cookie sheet, leaving a few inches between each. Repeat this process until you have enough to fill a baking sheet.

When the sheet is full, brush the bagels with the 2 yolks and water. Bake for 20 to 25 minutes.

Remove the bagels from the sheet onto racks to cool.

NOTE: Potato water is nothing more than the water you've drained after boiling potatoes. If you've forgotten to save some from the last batch of mashed potatoes, simply boil up a few potatoes right now.

The Recipe Holder

· The Recipe Holder ·

Although originally designed for mail, this basket is perfect for holding all the recipes you tear out of magazines and newspapers. Make this basket and hang it in a handy place, and you might just free up that catch-all kitchen drawer.

Tools

sharp scissors

tape measure

clothespins or spring clips

a 3- to 5-gallon dishpan or your
  kitchen sink

pocket knife or Surform Shaver

pencil

awl

Materials

From dyed ½-inch flat reed, 1 spoke
  30 inches long and 6 spokes
  23 inches long

From natural ½-inch flat reed,
  2 spokes 30 inches long and
  5 spokes 23 inches long

Approximately 70 inches ½-inch flat
  oval for rims

Approximately 30 inches sea grass

12 inches of #12 chair spline for
  handle

¼-inch flat oval, natural and dyed
  for weaving (approximately
  1 pound)

Finished basket measures 9^1/$_2$ inches x 6 inches x 8 inches high plus 2^1/$_2$ inches for the handle.

Preparation: Soak the spokes for five minutes in warm water. Mark the middle, wrong side of the long dyed spoke and the middle, wrong side of one natural shorter spoke.

The Base: Place the shorter middle-marked spoke vertically on your work surface. With middle marks matching, create a cross with the longer spoke on top being the horizontal member.

Weave a natural long spoke to the north, a dyed shorter spoke to the west, a long natural spoke to the south, and one more dyed shorter spoke to the east.

Everything is now locked.

Using the remaining spokes, to the east weave one natural, one dyed, one natural and one dyed. To the west weave one natural, one dyed, one natural and the last dyed spoke. Base measurements: 9 inches by 2^1/$_2$ inches.

When it's time to weave the sides, be sure to always put a coiled weaver into warm water whenever you take one out.

Creating the Sides: With the base flat on your work surface, you will work 2 rows from the inside and a third row from the outside. Then, with the sides bent up, all rows are worked from the outside.

With a soaked dyed ¼-inch weaver wrong side facing you, weave around the base, over one, under one.

At the corners, bring up the two corner spokes as you weave around them so that they are perpendicular to the base. Hold them in this position until you've woven at least two more spokes. When you let go, one corner spoke will stay up and the other will go down.

At the end of the row, overlap 4 spokes. (Throughout the basket, all rows are individual, as opposed to continuous weaving.)

On the other long side of the basket, weave another row in the same manner with a dyed weaver. This row will hold up the corner spoke not held previously. Flip the base over. Be sure all spokes are flattened out. With the *right side* of a natural weaver facing you, weave around the base. At the corners, hold the corner up from the working surface but have the spokes pointing downward and close to each other. Keep the weaver taut.

After this third row of weaving is complete, bend up the sides of the basket gently at the edge of the base.

Your main concern at this point is to be sure to splay out the three end spokes, while remembering to have the other spokes pointing straight up.

!!!!!   The 4th row of weaving will be natural and so will the 5th.   !!!!!

For the next 24 rows this is the pattern of weaving:

2 dyed   1 natural   2 dyed   3 natural

The 25th row is the false rim and will be natural.

Finishing Up: Cut off the inner spokes flush with the top of the basket. Cut the outer spokes long enough to tuck into at least 2 rows of weaving.

Soak the remaining spoke ends and tuck.

Making the Handle: With a 12-inch piece of chair spline, make a mark 2½ inches from the end on a curved side of the spline. Make another mark ½ inch above it. Do the same thing on the other end. This is where the notches will go.

On the inner flat side of your spline make a mark ¾ inch above the notch mark.

Repeat on other side.

Thin out the area between last 2 marks to about half the width of the spline.

Now make a mark ½ inch below the notch marks on the same curved edge of the spline.

Thin this down to slightly thicker than the spokes.

Soak the handle in warm water for about 20 minutes. Bend to shape. Cut out notches.

Inserting Handle: Insert the handle inside the basket. Start tucking at the 6th row of weaving following the 4th and 8th spokes with notches facing inside.

Rims: From ½ inch flat oval, cut 2 pieces the circumference of the basket, plus enough for about 4 inches of overlap. The inner rim should be about 2 inches shorter than the outer rim. Both rims should overlap in the same area but not on top of one another. After clipping on rims, insert sea grass as filler.

Lashing: Using ¼-inch flat oval, begin lashing just beyond the rim overlaps. This way they are the last parts to be lashed and any slack or tautness is easier to correct. Lash in whatever manner you've found comfortable.

Soup's On

Many years ago it was my pleasure to spend a week in Brittany with a marvelous Frenchwoman, who dazzled me with what she could accomplish in the tiny kitchen of her four-hundred-year-old house. My compliments to the chef were always met with "Oh, it's nothing. Just top of the stove."

When I receive praise for one of my "thrown together" soups, stews, or chowders I find myself quoting my hostess, Jacqueline Aillet, then end up sharing tales of this wonderful woman and the unforgettable week I spent with her.

She had no file of recipes and no collection of cookbooks. Every creation came out of her head, made with what was in her kitchen, her garden, or from a local market. She shopped daily, so everything was fresh and everything was wonderful.

The only way my soups resemble Mlle. Aillet's style of cooking is that I almost always use what I have on hand. However, the vegetable soup I make this week only vaguely resembles the one I made last week, and neither is like the soup I'll make next week. I blush to think of what my French hostess would have to say about these soups my American friends think are so good. And I find it almost embarrassing to put down specific directions. As you read my recipes, please remember that they are only guides. If there's an ingredient that is absolutely essential I'll let you know; otherwise, feel free to use more or less of almost anything.

Most cooks are in agreement about what constitutes a chowder, a stew, or a soup, but I'd feel neglectful if I didn't put it in my own words. *Soup* is a fairly clear broth with vegetables and, if you wish, meat or fish. *Stew* is quite similar, but the broth has been thickened. The broth of *chowder* is milk or cream. Then there are creamed or pureed soups that resemble very thick broth but that are much, much more when properly made. I love making all of them because every time I do, it's a new adventure.

Here's an abbreviated list of ingredients I'm rarely without.

barley	Cognac	sherry
bouillon cubes	garlic	turnips
brown rice	lentils	well-labeled bags of
carrots	parsnips	frozen vegetable water
celery	potatoes	or meat stock

When I first got the idea from Julia Child to make soup stock from the water drained from cooked vegetables, I ended up throwing it out because I never got around to using it. My intentions were good, but I made soup so seldom the stock went bad before it was used. After discarding one too many jars of soup starter, I hit on the idea of freezing all those dibs and dabs in plastic bags. (Half-thawed liquids are removed from plastic bags more easily than from glass jars.) On soup day, there you have it—soup stock as fresh as the day it was frozen, with all vitamins and flavor intact. Once you get into this saving habit, it becomes second nature.

Learning how to make a tasty soup is satisfying. Whether you live alone, there are two of you, you have a houseful of children, or you entertain a lot, knowing how to put together a good soup on short notice is a skill worth mastering. Serve a bowl of your own soup with homemade bread, rolls, or biscuits and the compliments will start pouring in. Now all you need learn is to look humble and say simply, "Oh, it's nothing. Just top of the stove."

· Corn Chowder ·

Makes about 6 cups (4 good-sized servings)

I was brought up in Boston during the Depression by a Catholic mother who was an avid Red Sox fan. During the summer, Fridays meant two things to her: Ladies' Day at Fenway Park (half-price admission for women) and something simple for supper, the day we didn't eat meat. (Evening meals were never called "dinner" at our house.) Once I was old enough, probably nine, she taught me to make the following chowder. This freed her to go to the ballpark. If Mom hadn't been a baseball fan, I mightn't have learned to cook until I was in my teens.

4 or 5 medium potatoes
½ teaspoon salt, or more to taste
1 can (12 ounces) evaporated milk
   (see Note)

1 can (16½ ounces) cream-style corn
1 tablespoon margarine or butter
Few grindings of black pepper

Start a kettle boiling with about 4 cups of water.

Peel the potatoes and cut them into whatever size cubes you fancy. (I happen to like tiny ones.) Put the potatoes in a medium saucepan and add enough boiling water to cover them by about 1 inch. Add the salt, turn the heat to medium, and boil the potatoes until they're tender, 7 to 12 minutes depending on the size of the cubes. Don't let them get mushy.

Pour the evaporated milk into the water and potatoes. Add the corn, margarine, pepper, and a bit more salt if you think it needs it.

Keep the pan over medium heat just until the margarine or butter has melted. Do not let it boil. Serve immediately.

NOTE: If you have an aversion to canned milk (in this case it adds richness) drain the potatoes and add regular milk and/or cream.

· Potato Soup ·

Makes 6 to 8 servings

My mother used to say it was her potato soup that won my father's heart. She never wrote down the recipe, and I never paid much attention to how she made it. This simple soup comes very close to tasting like the one she claimed made my father propose.

Although I use a blender to puree the potatoes and onion, a sieve, ricer, or food press will produce almost the same results (but require much more effort). When I was young I can remember eating this soup hot, but now I sometimes serve it chilled. Hot or chilled, serve it before the meal or as the main dish, with crackers or homemade Breadsticks (page 37), rather than with anything soft.

continued

4 tablespoons (½ stick) butter or
   margarine

3 medium onions, thinly sliced

3 or 4 celery stalks, finely chopped

4 medium potatoes, peeled and
   thinly sliced

1 quart chicken broth (canned or
   made from bouillon cubes)

2 cups heavy cream (see Note)

Salt and pepper to taste (optional)

Melt the butter or margarine in a large, heavy saucepan over medium heat. Once the fat sizzles, add the onions and celery and cook about 15 minutes, stirring now and then, until the onions are limp, but not browned.

Add the potatoes and broth and boil gently for about 15 minutes, until the potatoes are soft. Let the mixture cool for 30 minutes. (It is dangerous to puree a very hot mixture, which can erupt through the top of the blender, scalding you. Wait for the mixture to cool before pureeing.) Puree the mixture in a blender and return it to the saucepan. Add the cream and, if desired, some salt and pepper. Heat, but do not boil.

NOTE: Milk may be substituted if calories or cholesterol are a consideration, but the soup won't be as tasty.

• Cream of Carrot Soup •

Makes 6 to 8 servings

A rich soup made with cream and butter, this can be served either as a main dish or before the meal. If used as the former, start with a giant garden salad garnished with several kinds of cheese. Serve with a heaping basket of bran muffins and you have a well-rounded meal.

This recipe calls for a double boiler, which keeps the milk from boiling while allowing the rice to cook. If you don't have one, put the rice and milk in a medium saucepan and put this pan into a larger pan partly filled with boiling water.

1 cup white rice

4 cups milk

4 cups sliced carrots

4 cups chicken broth

¼ cup (½ stick) butter

4 medium onions, peeled and sliced

3 tablespoons all-purpose flour

1 tablespoon salt

¼ teaspoon pepper

1 cup heavy cream

½ to 1 cup milk (if needed)

In the top of a double boiler, combine the rice and milk and cook until the rice is tender, about 45 minutes.

Meanwhile, bring the carrots to a boil in the chicken broth and cook until they're tender, about 20 minutes. Do not drain. While the carrots are cooking, melt the butter in a medium frying pan and cook the onions until soft but not browned, about 20 minutes. Add the flour gradually along with the salt and pepper.

Combine the carrots, onions, and cooked rice in a bowl. When cool enough to be safe, in batches, puree in a blender. (It is dangerous to puree a very hot mixture. It can erupt through the top of the blender, scalding you. Wait for the mixture to cool before pureeing.) Return the soup to the saucepan and whisk in the cream. If the mixture seems too thick, use as much of the milk as necessary to thin it.

·Zucchini Soup·

Makes 4 generous servings

Since zucchini is so plentiful all summer in Vermont, I have six recipes for using it in soup. This is the best one. I usually serve it chilled, but one cold day in July (it was 42°F., no kidding), I served it hot and it was great. If you can stand to buy zucchini in the winter (remembering how much you gave away or were given just a few months ago), then by all means try this soup hot some cold winter evening. Serve it before the meal or as a main dish with plenty of Hearty Carrot Bread (page 45) and lots of cheddar cheese.

3 tablespoons corn oil

3 cups sliced zucchini (3 small
   zucchini or 2 medium)

1 medium onion, sliced

2 garlic cloves, minced

2 cups chicken bouillon

½ teaspoon salt

⅛ teaspoon pepper

1 cup milk

2 tablespoons cornstarch

1 cup heavy cream

¼ cup dry vermouth

¼ cup fresh dill, if available, or
   1 tablespoon dried dill

In a medium saucepan, heat the oil over medium heat and add the zucchini, onion, and garlic. Cook for about 10 minutes, stirring frequently until the onion is limp and the zucchini is soft.

Add the bouillon, salt, and pepper. Cover the pot, turn down the heat, and simmer for 15 minutes. Allow the mixture to cool for 30 minutes. (It is dangerous to puree a very hot mixture. It can erupt through the top of the blender, scalding you. Wait for the mixture to cool before pureeing.) Puree the mixture in batches in a blender and return to the saucepan over low heat.

Carefully combine the milk and cornstarch into a smooth mixture and add the cream. Pour the cream mixture into the saucepan, stirring constantly. Bring the soup to a boil, and boil for 1 minute. Add the vermouth and dill and stir well. Remove the soup from the heat and chill several hours or overnight.

Just before serving, stir well with a wire whisk to be sure everything is well blended.

·Onion Soup·

Makes 8 servings

This is a dinner party soup. Dress it up with croutons and grated cheddar cheese, and present it before the main course.

4 tablespoons (½ stick) butter
1½ tablespoons olive oil
2 pounds yellow onions, thinly sliced
    (about 6 cups)
1 teaspoon salt
½ teaspoon sugar
3 tablespoons all-purpose flour
2 quarts beef broth (canned or made
    from bouillon cubes)

½ cup dry vermouth
2 tablespoons Cognac
Salt and pepper to taste
    (optional)
2 cups (½ pound) grated cheddar
    cheese
3 or 4 cups Croutons (page 190)

Heat the butter and oil in a large, heavy saucepan (a Dutch oven is ideal) until the butter starts to bubble. Add the onions and cook over low heat, covered, for about 15 onions, stirring occasionally, until very soft.

Add the salt and sugar, increase the heat to moderate, and cook uncovered for 40 to 45 minutes, until a uniform caramel color. Keep your eye on the onions, stirring them frequently; browning is important, but burning is unacceptable.

Bring the broth to a boil. When the onions are browned and reduced to about one-fifth their original volume, sprinkle in the flour and stir for several minutes to cook the flour. (If you have an electric range, turn the burner off. The heat that remains will be sufficient. With a gas range, turn the flame as low as it will go.)

Remove the pot from the heat and stir in the boiling broth and vermouth. Return the pot to a low heat and, with the lid tipped, simmer the soup for about 45 minutes longer. You may want to add salt and pepper at this point, but I rarely do.

Pour the soup into a tureen, and stir in the Cognac.

Fill each bowl at the table, then pass the cheese and croutons and let guests serve themselves.

• Vegetable-Beef Stew •

Makes 6 to 8 servings

On a snowy, cold winter's evening, or a drizzling, chilly day in early spring or late autumn you need something hot inside you—something nourishing—something to make you feel good about life in general. This is the stew that will do the trick.

There are two sets of ingredients listed: the essential and the optional. Remember, above all, that this is your stew and my instructions are just guidelines.

continued

1½ pounds stew beef

1 cup seasoned flour, for dredging
(see Note)

4 tablespoons olive oil

2 medium onions, thinly sliced

4 or 5 garlic cloves, finely chopped

2 quarts beef broth (canned or made
from bouillon cubes)

1 tablespoon salt

3 tablespoons barley

3 tablespoons lentils

1 small turnip, peeled and diced

2 medium carrots, peeled and diced

2 medium potatoes, peeled and
diced

2 medium parsnips, peeled and
diced

1 tablespoon dried basil or 3 tablespoons chopped fresh

4 tablespoons (½ stick) butter

4 tablespoons all-purpose flour

¼ teaspoon ground pepper

Optional Additions

Handful of cut-up green beans

1 small green bell pepper, diced

½ cup fresh or frozen peas

2 celery stalks, thinly sliced

Cut the beef into bite-size pieces and dredge in seasoned flour.

In a large, heavy saucepan, heat the oil until a drop of water will
sizzle in it. Add the beef and cook over medium-high heat, stirring
to turn all the pieces until they are uniformly browned, about 10
minutes. Be careful not to burn the beef during this process.

Reduce the heat to medium, add the onions and garlic, and cook
until wilted but not browned, about 10 minutes. The onions and garlic will have picked up some color from the beef, but it is not necessary to *cook* them brown.

Pour in the broth and bring to a boil. Add the salt, barley, and lentils, reduce the heat, and simmer until the meat is tender, about 2½ hours.

At 5-minute intervals, add the turnip, carrots, potatoes, and parsnips. (By adding the vegetables in this order, they will all be finished cooking at the same time.) Finally, add the basil. Turn down the heat and allow the vegetables and meat to simmer. If you are adding any of the optional vegetables (all of which cook quickly), now is the time to do so.

When the vegetables are cooked (about 10 minutes after the last ones are added), it's time to thicken the stew. In a small dish, rub together, either with your fingers or the back of a spoon, the flour and butter—the French call this a *beurre manie*. Form the mixture into a ball and stir it into the stew until it dissolves. The broth will thicken slightly and the stew will take on the special opulent flavor that only a *beurre manie* can impart. Add pepper to taste.

NOTE: Add 2 teaspoons salt and ¼ teaspoon ground pepper to 1 cup of flour and you have seasoned flour for dredging, which simply means to cover the meat lightly with the flour (easily accomplished by putting both flour and meat in a plastic bag and shaking well).

The One That Got Away

(Or Why I Can't Tell You How to Make P.I. Soup)

As a child summering in Maine, my brothers and sister, my cousins, and I always knew that if we had supper at Maimie's (our grandmother's house), it would be baked beans or P.I. Soup, and plenty of freshly baked homemade bread. It was always open house to her nine children and several dozen grandchildren. No one needed an invitation. If you were there at mealtime, it was assumed you would stay and eat. My grandmother must have made other things, but all I remember is her homemade bread, baked beans, and P.I. Soup.

P.I. stood for Prince Edward Island, the province in Canada where my grandparents were born. And the soup that bore its name was the best. In my youth it never occurred to me to ask how something was made. I just savored it and knew there was always more where it came from.

When it was my turn to cook for a family, I tried many times to duplicate that great P.I. Soup, but something was always lacking. Those who ate my non–P.I. Soup were satisfied, but not I. After many trials I gave up and just made soup-soup, the kind I could throw together from what I had on hand. Every once in a while I'd think about writing to one of my aunts to see if she knew how to make that elusive treat, but I never carried through.

When the children were young I liked to treat them to restaurant fare now and then. I thought it important they understand that eating out meant more than hamburgers, French fries, and a shake. I'd heard about a restaurant whose salad bar was an ice-filled bathtub and thought this would tickle the kids. It was lunch time and they were convinced they could satisfy their appetites dipping into the tub. I decided to sample the lentil soup along with half a sandwich.

With my first spoonful I was in heaven—or to be more precise, I was back in Maine, a kid again, sitting at Maimie's table once more. When I beckoned our waiter, his first reaction was to ask if there was anything wrong.

"No, no," I said excitedly. "This soup is incredible. It tastes exactly like what my grandmother used to make. I've been trying to duplicate it for years. Do you think the chef would share the recipe with me?"

He headed for the kitchen and we saw no more of him until it was time to order dessert.

"Well, what did the chef say?" I asked eagerly.

"I'll ask him again," he answered, in a voice that had an edge to it.

When we were finally presented with the check, I pressed the poor waiter once more for an answer regarding the soup recipe. Bending down to whisper in my ear, he said, "You must never tell anyone this, but on Mondays he uses canned soup. It's Progresso."

I bought some on my way home, but it didn't taste the same. He must have doctored it some way.

I decided to get serious about this P.I. Soup. Why had I waited so long to go to the source? I put in a call to my aunt, Leah Coleman, who still lives in Bath, Maine. I literally begged her to tell me how she made that soup we all enjoyed so much at Maimie's house. I took down her instructions very carefully, and I did everything she told me to do, but much to my disappointment it didn't taste the way I remembered. Oh, it was a good soup, but not the P.I. Soup of my youth.

Was the taste of that long ago soup improved by the aroma of my grandfather's pipe? Did the sound of a cribbage game in the background make it taste better? I guess a cook trying to resurrect the flavors of childhood is like a fisherman describing the one that got away.

• Lamb Stew •

Makes 8 to 10 servings

New Englanders are notoriously frugal. Most old-time Vermonters know the saying "Use it up; wear it out; make it do or do without." This recipe for lamb stew is a perfect example of "use it up" philosophy. When I was growing up, the bones from a roast leg of lamb were always used for stew. These days if I want to serve roast lamb but know I won't have time to make a stew, I ease my conscience by having the butcher bone and roll the roast for me.

What some people don't like about lamb stew is the grease. This recipe is outstanding because it's grease free, *guaranteed*, if you carefully follow my directions. This means starting the stew in the morning to allow enough time for proper degreasing.

You can use more than the vegetables listed. I frequently add turnip, parsnip, or potato—or all three.

Leftover bones from roast leg of
  lamb
1 large onion, quartered
2 garlic cloves
2 teaspoons summer savory
1 tablespoon dried basil

2 tablespoons chopped fresh parsley
1 can (16-ounce) tomatoes
2 large carrots, peeled and sliced
½ cup dried split green peas
¼ cup barley
Salt and pepper to taste

continued

In a large, heavy stockpot over medium heat, cook the lamb bones (and any leftover lamb you may have carved off the roast and not used) in about a quart of water along with the onion, garlic, savory, and basil. When all the meat has fallen off, remove the bones.

Chill the broth completely. This may take 2 to 3 hours. The grease from the bones and meat must be *hardened* on top of the broth before you attempt to remove it.

Remove the hardened grease, then reheat the broth and add the parsley, tomatoes, carrots, split peas, and barley. Boil gently for about 1½ hours. The split peas and barley will thicken the broth, which is why this is a stew, not a soup. If you are adding other vegetables, do so during the last half-hour of cooking. Season with salt and pepper.

• Cream of Peanut Soup •

Makes 4 servings

The first time my daughter, the vegetarian, served this soup I was a bit skeptical; after my first taste I was ready for the recipe. It's quick and easy, and has several variations. Try each to see which you like best. Minus the sherry and plus the whipped cream, it's a real kid-pleaser and a nutritious lunch served with bread or crackers. If you feel like doubling the recipe, go right ahead. Any extra will freeze nicely.

1 tablespoon butter or margarine

½ tablespoon all-purpose flour

½ cup smooth peanut butter

2 cups milk

½ teaspoon salt

¼ cup sherry (optional)

½ cup peanuts and/or whipped
cream, for garnish

Over low heat, melt the butter in a medium saucepan. Stir in the flour and remove the pan from the heat. Blend in the peanut butter and add the milk gradually, stirring all the while. Return the soup to low heat and stir constantly until it's hot and steamy. Don't let it boil. Add the salt and sherry, if you're using it. Serve immediately and garnish the soup once it's in the bowls.

• Chilled Blueberry Soup •

Makes 4 servings

A lovely opener for a summer dinner party. Complete the menu with Potato Salad and Deviled Eggs (page 196) and a platter of cold cuts. Plan on a simple sherbet or ice cream for dessert.

2½ cups fresh blueberries

2 tablespoons honey

1 tablespoon lemon juice

1 teaspoon lemon zest

½ cup heavy cream

4 tablespoons plain yogurt, for
garnish (optional)

continued

Bring the blueberries, honey, lemon juice, and zest to a boil over medium heat in a medium saucepan, stirring constantly.

Reduce the heat to low and cook 5 minutes longer. Let the mixture cool for 30 minutes. (It is dangerous to puree a very hot mixture. It can erupt through the top of the blender, scalding you. Wait for the mixture to cool before pureeing.) Once cool, puree the mixture in a blender and chill thoroughly.

Add the cream just before serving. If you choose, once the soup is in the bowls you can make an attractive swirling design on top of each with a tablespoon of yogurt.

The Casserole Carrier

· The Casserole Carrier ·

Carrying a casserole in the car can be a tricky chore. That's how I came to design this handy carrying basket. Big enough for a 3-quart casserole, it can also accommodate a 10-inch pie.

With its sturdy open side handles and filled bottom you're assured this basket is strong enough to safely hold anything that fits into it. (Note: Kits are available. See Mail Order Sources, page 200.)

Tools

sharp scissors

tape measure

clothespins or spring clips

a 3- to 5-gallon dishpan or your
    kitchen sink

pencil

awl

Materials

From ⅝-inch flat reed, 22 spokes
    25 inches long

From ⅜-inch flat reed, 10 fillers
    17 inches long

½ pound ⅜-inch flat reed for
    weavers

Approximately 35 feet #3 or #4
    round reed

Approximately 3 yards ½-inch flat
    oval (for rims)

Approximately 5 feet sea grass
    (for filler)

Approximately 8 yards ¼-inch flat
    oval for lashing

Finished dimensions: 11 inches by 11
    inches by 4 inches high

Preparation: Soak the spokes for at least 5 minutes in warm water before using. With a pencil, number the spokes 1 through 22 on the wrong side. Mark the middle of spokes 1 and 2 on the *right* side. Mark the middle of one filler spoke on the *wrong* side.

The Base: Place spoke 1 right side facing you, vertically on the work surface. Place spoke 2 right side facing you, on top of it, horizontally, middle marks aligned, forming a cross.

For the remainder of the base, remember to place *spokes right side up* and *fillers wrong side up.*

With the wrong side facing up, place the marked filler, vertically, to the east of spoke 1 and overlapping spoke 2.

Place another filler, vertically, to the west of spoke 1, lined up with the first filler. All fillers are wrong side up and aligned and must touch adjoining spokes. The space between horizontals should be ⅜ inch.

Working to the north of spoke 2, weave in spokes 3, 4, 5, 6, and 7.

Working to the south of spoke 2, weave in spokes 8, 9, 10, 11, and 12.

You now have 11 horizontal spokes woven through 1 vertical spoke and 2 fillers.

Give your base one turn clockwise so that the horizontals become verticals.

Bend the fillers up and tuck the ends under the third spoke from the end, cutting off any portion that extends beyond the third spoke.

Working toward the north, and starting with spoke 13, weave in a spoke and then a filler. Remember that fillers go in wrong side facing up. Tuck in ends of fillers each time, until you have spokes 13 through 17 and 5 fillers alternating to the north of the middle-marked spoke. All spokes and fillers touching.

Using spokes 18 through 22, repeat this process to the south.

Base should measure 11 inches by 11 inches. Flip it over so that the wrong sides of the spokes are facing you and the tucked fillers are resting on the work surface. (When it's time to weave the sides, always be sure to put one coiled weaver in warm water whenever you take one out.)

Creating the Sides: With the base flat on your work surface, you will work 2 rows from the inside and a third row from the outside. Then, with the sides bent up, all rows are worked from the outside. With the wrong side facing you, place the end of a soaked 3/8-inch flat oval weaver on top of spoke 5 with the tip of the weaver lining up with the left-hand side of the spoke. Going from left to right, weave under spoke 4, over spoke 3, under spoke 2, etc., until you reach the corner.

At the corners, bend up spokes 12 and 17 so that they are perpendicular to the work surface. Weave in front of spoke 12 and behind spoke 17. Spoke 12 will flop down, while spoke 17 will remain upright.

Weave to the next corner. Bend up spokes 22 and 12. Weave behind spoke 22 and in front of spoke 12. Spoke 12 will go down and 22 will remain upright. On the third corner, spoke 7 will remain up while spoke 22 goes down, and on the fourth corner, spoke 17 will remain up while spoke 7 goes down.

To end this row, and all rows that follow, overlap the weaver for 4 spokes, cut it, and hide it behind the fourth spoke.

Give the base one turn clockwise. Start weaving on any over spoke near the middle. When you weave this row, you will be holding up the corner spokes not held up previously.

Flip the base over and make sure that all spokes are flat. With the right side of the weaver facing you, start weaving on the opposite side of the base.

When you reach the corner, hold it up from the work surface, but have your spokes pointing downward and close to each other. The remainder of the base stays flat on the work surface. Keep the weaver taut while you weave around the 2 corner spokes. Keep the other spokes flat on the work surface as you weave them. Only the corners come up.

Bend up the sides of the basket at the edge of the base. Weave until your basket is 3 inches high.

Cut 3 lengths of round reed, approximately 2¼ times the circumference of the basket, and put them to soak in lukewarm water.

On opposite sides of the basket, starting all the way to the corner, mark the top of your spokes 1 to 7 (erase any existing marks).

You will now proceed to make a 3-rod arrow.

Insert one weaver behind spoke 5, another behind spoke 6, and the third weaver behind spoke 7. The farthest left weaver goes *in front of* two spokes, *above* the right two weavers, *behind* the next spoke, and then *out*.

Repeat this sequence all the way around your basket until you have weavers coming out from behind spokes 2, 3, and 4.

(For additional information on this technique, as well as excellent diagrams, see Flo Hoppe's book, *Wicker Basketry*, Interweave Press, 201 East 4th Street, Loveland, Colorado 80537.)

Working from left to right, refer to the weavers that come out from behind spokes **2, 3** and **4** as: x y and z

Pick up weaver z. Weave in front of 2 spokes, behind the next spoke, and out. Pick up weaver y and repeat the process. Finally, pick up weaver x and repeat the process once more.

The farthest left weaver now goes in front of 2 spokes, *under* the right two weavers, behind the next spoke, and then out. Continue this sequence until the weavers come out from behind spokes 2, 3, and 4 one more time.

Once more, going from left to right, refer to your weavers as x, y, and z. Pick up z; weave it in front of 2 spokes, and as you bring it into the basket, behind the next spoke, insert it under the top 2 weavers.

Pick up weaver y and repeat the previous process. Finally, pick up weaver x and repeat the process once more. Cut off excess weaver ends.

If your spokes have dried out, wet the 3 middle spokes on opposite sides, bend them down into the basket, and tuck them into 2 weavers.

Row 1 (above round reed): Working from left to right, tuck the beginning of your weaver behind the first 3 spokes to the right of your handle opening. Weave the back and front together for 3 spokes (this will use up the inner weaver) and hide it behind the third spoke. Weave normally until you reach the other handle opening. Leave enough weaver to bend behind three spokes. Weave the end in. Repeat this process on the other side of the second handle opening.

Row 2: This row of weaving is done in the same manner, except that it starts on the second spoke in.

Row 3: Follow directions for Row 1.

Weave a complete row around the top of the basket. When you get to the handle openings, be sure to weave under the spokes on both sides of the opening.

Finishing Up: Cut off the inner spokes flush with the top of the basket. Cut the outer spokes long enough to tuck into at least 2 rows of weaving.

Soak the remaining spoke ends and tuck.

Rims: From ½-inch flat oval, cut 2 pieces the circumference of the basket, plus enough for about 4 inches of overlap. The inner rim should be about 2 inches shorter than the outer rim.

Both rims should overlap in the same area but not on top of one another. After clipping on rims, insert sea grass as filler.

Lashing: Using ¼-inch flat oval, begin lashing just beyond the rim overlaps. This way they are the last parts to be lashed and any slack or tautness is easier to correct. Lash in whatever manner you've found comfortable.

Casseroles for All Occasions

You'll like the versatility of the casseroles in this chapter. Every one can be a main dish with salad and/or meat accompanying it. Rahtatooee (page 89), Tomato Bisque (page 88), and Baked Lima Beans (page 90) are certainly more interesting than peas or carrots to serve with meat and potato. And Zapikanka (page 94) and Escalloped Cheese (page 86) are appropriate for filling out almost any menu.

Except for Zapikanka, which you can whip up in a jiffy, and Kohlrabi Chicken Soufflé (page 97), all of these casseroles can be made ahead of time, removing a lot of pressure if timing plays an important part in your plans.

Although it wasn't intentional, most of the casseroles are meatless. This makes them particularly good choices for a variety of reasons. They're healthful, economical, and the perfect buffet alternative for vegetarians, or on Fridays during Lent for the Catholics among us.

· Escalloped Cheese ·

Makes 4 main-dish servings or 8 side-dish servings

This recipe came to me by way of my son-in-law's grandmother, Marilla Smith. I make it at least once a month for the ten retired ladies for whom I cook supper at the Gary Home for the Aged, in Montpelier. Given their way, they'd have me make it once a week. It's their all-time favorite (even edging out Vichyssoise). The ladies of the Gary Home know it as Bread and Cheese Soufflé, but daughter Julia said I could not include it in my book unless I used the name of the original recipe.

Regardless of what you call it, timing is important if you're serving this to guests: it must be put on the table the moment it comes out of the oven. Like all soufflés (*which it is!*), it doesn't take long to deflate.

8 slices bread
Approximately 3 tablespoons
    margarine
4 eggs
1 quart milk

½ teaspoon salt
½ teaspoon dry mustard
2 cups grated cheddar cheese
    (½ pound)

Grease a 2-quart casserole and preheat the oven to 350°F.

Spread each piece of bread with about a teaspoon of margarine. Cut the bread into ½-inch cubes and set aside.

In a medium bowl, beat together the eggs, milk, salt, and mustard.

Into the greased casserole place half the bread cubes, sprinkle half the cheese over the bread, arrange the rest of the bread cubes over the cheese, and top with the remaining cheese. Pour the egg and milk mixture over the bread and cheese, and let it stand for at least 20 minutes, allowing the bread to absorb the liquid.

Bake for 35 minutes or until it has risen quite high and is beautifully browned. Serve immediately.

NOTE: Since the ladies at the Gary Home have their main meal (dinner) at noon, this casserole is always served as an evening (supper) dish accompanied by a Waldorf salad or Tomato Aspic (page 189). And since Julia is a vegetarian, she, too, serves it as a main dish, usually with a giant salad. There's no reason, however, not to serve it as a side dish for dinner along with, let's say, pork chops and applesauce or meat loaf and a vegetable.

·Tomato Bisque with Two Cheeses·

Makes 4 generous servings

Here's an inexpensive, simple lunch or supper you can whip up in jig time. If you're making it for two, just halve the recipe. If you live alone, use one small can of tomatoes and quarter the recipe. Single servings can be heated in a microwave. Because it contains starch, protein, and vegetable, this is a complete meal, needing nothing to accompany it but a good book (if you're eating alone) or a pleasant companion (if you're lucky enough to have one).

I've included this recipe here because ordinarily it gets baked for a while. However, on many a hot July evening I've concocted this

2 cans (16 ounces each) stewed
  tomatoes
8 ounces crackers, crumbled (round
  milk biscuits work and taste best)

8 ounces cottage cheese
1 cup shredded cheddar cheese

bisque and eaten it cold.

Preheat the oven to 375°F.

In no particular order, mix all the ingredients in a bowl. Place in a greased 2-quart casserole and bake 45 minutes.

• Rahtatooee •

Makes 12 servings

This recipe is my take-off on that French classic ratatouille (phonetically spelled for my recipe to not confuse the two). The basic ingredients are all here, but the assembly is strictly my own. Serve with roast meat and potato, as a baked potato topping, or on pasta (my favorite way of serving it).

Although I give specific amounts for each ingredient, feel free to alter them as you please. The first time around you might want to do it my way, but then adapt it to suit your tastes. Like my soups, my Rahtatooee rarely comes out the same way twice.

Don't be intimidated by the large amount this recipe makes. You can freeze what's left in individual or family-size servings. It's a versatile dish to have on hand.

2 medium onions
4 garlic cloves
4 large mushrooms
4 tablespoons vegetable oil
1 large green bell pepper
2 medium zucchini
1 medium eggplant, peeled
2 cans (16 ounces each) tomatoes

1 tablespoon salt
½ teaspoon black pepper
¼ cup sugar
1 tablespoon dried basil, or 6 fresh
    basil leaves, snipped
1 tablespoon oregano (optional)
1 teaspoon chili powder

continued

Slice the onions, garlic, and mushrooms thinly. Heat the oil in a large, heavy pot (a Dutch oven works very well). Add the onions, garlic, and mushrooms and sauté until tender but not browned, about 10 minutes. Turn the heat to very low while you cut into ¾-inch cubes the green pepper, zucchini, and eggplant. (You are not expected to get out a ruler for this. I settled on ¾-inch because half-inch cubes seem too small and 1 inch a little large.) Add the raw vegetables to the sautéed ones in the pot and stir to mix.

Add the tomatoes, salt, pepper, sugar, basil, oregano if using, and chili powder.

Turn the heat to medium and cook until the mixture starts to boil, then reduce the heat and simmer for about 2 hours. This will cook all the vegetables and blend the flavors. (If I'm not baking anything else, or need to free up the top of my stove, I sometimes put the dish in a 350°F. oven to finish cooking.) Serve it in any of the ways suggested above or invent your own uses.

•Baked Lima Beans•

Makes 8 servings

Though not a dish to be served to the calorie conscious, this casserole is always a crowd pleaser. The lima beans need to soak at least eight hours before being cooked for an hour, and its takes ninety minutes for the casserole to bake, so this is not a spur-of-the-moment undertaking. Now that I've given you two *negatives*, you should have a *positive* attitude about putting this dish together. It is *yummy!* Baked ham or Canadian bacon goes very nicely with this casserole, and don't forget a nice tossed salad for contrast.

1 pound dried lima beans

1 tablespoon salt

½ cup (1 stick) butter or margarine, melted

1 cup sour cream

2 tablespoons molasses

2 teaspoons dry mustard

Soak the beans overnight or for 8 hours in about 4 quarts of cold water in a large, heavy pot. Do not drain (you lose some of the nutrients if you do). Add the salt, bring the beans to a boil, cover the pot, and reduce the heat. Cook for about 30 minutes or until tender, adding more water if needed. (A trick I learned from my mother—and even as I write this I can see her in our old kitchen doing it—to tell if the beans are done is to place a few on a spoon and blow on them. If the skin curls up, they're done. Either eat the tested beans or discard them.)

Preheat the oven to 300°F.

Mix the cooked beans, butter, sour cream, molasses, and dry mustard and pour the mixture into a casserole. Cover the casserole and bake for 1½ hours. Serve.

My Grandfather, the Alchemist

In the back kitchen of the big house on Willow Street in Bath, Maine, my grandfather made cottage cheese. At the bottom of the stairs, a white cloth bag hung over a soapstone sink, dripping whey into a chipped enamel basin. Something wonderful was lurking inside that white shroud, but the odor was awful. My grandfather, the alchemist, turned dreaded "gone by" milk into something tangy and wholesome, and he assured us grandchildren, something that was "good for us." My cousins took him at his word, and gobbled up his cottage cheese, but not I.

I loved my grandfather, and I wanted to believe him. But I couldn't get past the smell.

Couldn't, but had to. The only way to reach my upstairs bedroom was to pass through the back kitchen and up the back stairs. Grandchildren couldn't use the carpeted front stairway. With our grassy feet—one of the uncles had always just mowed the lawn—we were banished to the back. Several times a day I went through the back kitchen, past the bag of curd, and up the back stairs. Why did my beloved grandfather have to hang his dreadful cottage cheese in that particular spot? Each time I went by I held my nose, unless of course my grandfather was there. With great effort I kept my hands behind my back lest I offend him. Of course, if my grandfather was in the area, so was the pungent aroma of his pipe smoke, which managed to cover up the sharp smell wafting from the sink.

As hard as he tried, my grandfather could not get me to taste the cottage cheese he was so proud of. Love has its boundaries. Sampling something that smelled so foul being made was a leap I couldn't take. Many years later, I gave cottage cheese a try. Much to my surprise I enjoyed it. I started to use it on and in almost anything. I totally forgot that smelly cloth bag hanging over the sink in Maine.

So I thought, until the day I took my children to see how cheese and butter were made at the Cabot Creamery. Sniffing my way through those corridors took me back—back to my grandfather's back kitchen. It was the smell of curds and whey: cottage cheese in the making.

Instead of being overwhelmed by loathsome images, to my astonishment the aroma brought back only pleasant memories. The odor of the creamery evoked a vivid remembrance of how much I loved and admired my grandfather, the alchemist, who could turn "gone by" milk into something "good for us."

·Zapikanka·

(Something for Supper, from Russia with Love)

Makes 4 servings

In the summer of 1992 I spent two weeks in Russia with a group of Vermont artisans. Each was assigned to a host family, and the Korshakovas got me.

Despite terrible food shortages and high prices at that time, Marina Korshakova had a well-stocked freezer. Her meals were bountiful and beautifully prepared. Near the end of my visit, however, the freezer was finally empty. Marina's plan was to buy a chicken on our way home from the Children's Palace of Creativity, where she taught Karelian embroidery and I taught basketry. At three shops, while Marina checked out the chicken, I stood in line. Either the birds did not look good, the price was too high, or she could see that when we reached the counter the chicken would be sold out.

I assured her it wasn't necessary to cook meat every night. She could put together something simple. We were good enough friends at this point not to treat me as "company." I knew no Russian and her English was sketchy, but I got the point across. Marina made a casserole; her husband, Jayna, prepared salad. With beautiful black bread and fresh creamery butter, one could not have wished for anything better. "A peasant's meal," she apologized. Lucky peasants, thought I.

Marina's casserole recipe went into my trip diary, and each time I make it I say a silent *spacibo* (thank-you) to my good Russian friend.

2 cups cottage cheese
2 eggs
½ cup unbleached all-purpose flour
2 tablespoons sugar

½ teaspoon ground cinnamon
¼ teaspoon salt
Pinch of baking soda

Preheat the oven to 350°F. Grease a 1-quart casserole.

In a bowl, combine the cottage cheese, eggs, flour, sugar, cinnamon, salt, and baking soda. Pour the mixture into the casserole and bake for 20 minutes.

Raise the heat to 425°F. and bake 15 to 20 minutes longer. The casserole should be brown on top and should not wiggle. Test it by inserting a knife in the middle. When you press the knife gently to one side, the casserole should be set—no longer liquid—the consistency of baked custard.

•Chicken-Cantaloupe Cold Casserole•

Makes 6 servings

Vermonters make the most of their short growing season, frequently putting in second and third plantings of lettuce and radish, and whenever possible, a second planting of peas. Here's a great main-dish casserole to serve on a late summer evening. Except for a few of the dressing ingredients, I can get everything, including the chicken, at my farmers' market in Montpelier the first or second week of September.

Breadsticks (page 37) make an excellent accompaniment to this main-dish casserole.

2 large boneless chicken breasts

2 cups chicken broth

4 cups chopped fresh spinach
   (1 pound)

2 cups diced cantaloupe
   (1 melon)

½ cup sliced celery (1 stalk)

½ cup sliced radishes

1 cup shelled green peas

2 tablespoons minced onion

2 tablespoons minced fresh parsley

2 garlic cloves, halved (see Note)

½ cup grated cheddar cheese

Juice and zest of 1 lemon

½ cup plain yogurt

1 tablespoon tarragon wine vinegar

2 tablespoons maple syrup

½ teaspoon salt

Freshly ground pepper

In a medium saucepan, simmer the chicken breasts in the broth for 15 or 20 minutes, until just tender. Drain and cool. While the chicken is cooling, prepare and place the spinach, cantaloupe, celery, radishes, peas, onion, and parsley in a large casserole.

Cut the chicken into bite-size cubes and toss with the ingredients in the bowl. Position the garlic cloves strategically throughout.

To make the dressing, combine the cheese, lemon zest and juice, yogurt, vinegar, maple syrup, and salt and pepper in a food processor or blender and puree, until smooth.

Just before serving, remove the pieces of garlic and pour the dressing over all.

NOTE: Skewer each garlic half with a toothpick, to make it easier to find when it's time to remove it.

•Kohlrabi Chicken Soufflé•

Makes 6 servings

Kohlrabi, the strange-looking vegetable that looks like a cross between a cabbage and a turnip, and tastes like a combination of the two, goes nicely with chicken in this easy-to-put-together soufflé. Serve it with a fresh garden salad for a nutritionally balanced meal that will taste as good as it looks. *continued*

3 medium kohlrabi, peeled and
   diced
2 medium potatoes, peeled and
   diced
2 tablespoons margarine or
   vegetable oil
1 large boned chicken breast, cut
   into bite-size pieces
2 tablespoons minced onion

1 tablespoon minced fresh parsley
½ teaspoon dried savory
¼ teaspoon paprika
½ teaspoon Worcestershire sauce
6 eggs, separated
2 tablespoons all-purpose flour
½ cup grated cheese
½ teaspoon salt
Few grindings of black pepper

Grease a shallow 1½-quart casserole. Preheat the oven to 325°F.

Steam the kohlrabi about 5 minutes, until just tender. Boil the potatoes about 8 minutes, also until just tender.

Heat the margarine to a sizzle in a medium frying pan and sauté the chicken, onion, parsley, savory, and paprika. It should take only 6 or 7 minutes for the chicken to be tender and no longer pink. Stir in the Worcestershire sauce.

In a large bowl, stir together the kohlrabi, potatoes, and chicken with herbs. In a small bowl, whisk together the egg yolks and flour, then fold into the kohlrabi mixture. Add the cheese, salt, and pepper.

Beat the egg whites and fold them into the kohlrabi mixture. Carefully spoon everything into the prepared baking dish and bake for about 45 minutes or until the top is a lovely golden hue. Serve immediately.

·Whole Stuffed Cabbage·

Makes 6 to 8 servings

High in protein, high in fiber, and very flavorful, the only thing this casserole lacks is ease of preparation. Although it's time-consuming, the dish is almost foolproof to prepare. Plan on plenty of time. The brown rice alone takes forty-five minutes to cook. Since the cabbage needs to cook for ten minutes and then cool for another ten minutes for ease of handling, start the cabbage, lentils, and rice at the same time but in separate pots. During this time, dice and grate the ingredients that need it. You may still have time to make the tomato sauce topping while the rice finishes cooking. Or you can do it once the stuffing is put together—a simple five-minute process. The whole process takes a minimum of two hours, but you're going to *love* this dish!

Hints

- *Use only a Savoy cabbage. Red and green cabbage leaves are not pliant enough.*
- *You'll need 1 cup of cooked brown rice. Bring 3 cups of water and ½ teaspoon of salt to a boil. Add ⅓ cup brown rice, reduce heat, cover, and simmer for 45 minutes or until the rice is tender and all the water is absorbed.*

continued

- *Lentils double in bulk when cooked. Since you'll need 2 cups of cooked lentils, add 1 cup of rinsed lentils to 3 cups lightly salted boiling water. Reduce heat and simmer approximately 30 minutes or until the lentils are tender. If all the water is not absorbed, drain the lentils.*
- *The simplest way to peel tomatoes is to immerse them for about 45 seconds in boiling water, then run cold water over them. This loosens the skin, which then can be removed easily.*

⅓ cup brown rice

1 cup lentils

1 medium Savoy cabbage

3 medium carrots, grated

1 medium onion, finely chopped

2 medium tomatoes, peeled and finely chopped

1 cup grated cheddar cheese

⅓ cup slivered almonds

3 medium figs, finely chopped

2 eggs, slightly beaten

8 to 10 fresh basil leaves, minced, or 2 tablespoons dried basil

Juice and zest of 1 lemon

1½ teaspoons ground cinnamon

For Sauce

1 tablespoon olive oil

1 cup diced onion

1½ cups tomato puree

Scant ½ teaspoon ground cinnamon

1 tablespoon maple syrup

Salt and pepper to taste

Start cooking the rice and the lentils. See Hints. Boil the cabbage for 10 minutes in just enough water to cover it. Remove the cabbage from the boiling water, taking care not to tear the outer leaves. Place in a colander and run cold water over to stop the cooking. Drain well.

Cut the stem of the cabbage so that it will sit flat and place it, stem side down, in an ovenproof bowl that just fits it. Being careful not to tear the leaves, peel them back until you get to the center. Set aside.

Check the lentils; they should be cooked by now. When the rice is ready, pour it into a medium bowl and add the lentils, carrots, onion, tomatoes, cheese, almonds, figs, eggs, basil, lemon juice and zest, and cinnamon. Stir until well blended, then divide into 4 equal portions.

Cut out the core and enough inner leaves of the cabbage to accommodate one-fourth of the stuffing. Fill with 1 portion of stuffing, then fold over a layer of leaves to cover the filling. Pack another one-fourth of the stuffing over these leaves, and cover it with another layer of leaves. Do this 2 more times, using up the stuffing and folding over all remaining leaves of cabbage so that all the stuffing is covered.

Preheat the oven to 350°F.

Heat the oil for the sauce in a small saucepan and sauté the onion until limp but not brown, about 10 minutes. Add the tomato puree, cinnamon, maple syrup, salt, and pepper. Pour the sauce over the cabbage and cover the bowl with a piece of aluminum foil, being sure it doesn't touch the cabbage. Bake for 45 minutes.

Remove the cabbage from the oven and let sit, uncovered, for 10 minutes. Carefully transfer the cabbage to a large platter and slice into wedge-shaped pieces for serving.

Meal's End

As far as I'm concerned, the perfect way to end any meal is with ice cream. But even ice cream pales now and then. When something with pizzazz is called for, any of these desserts will fill the bill.

I think of Baked Alaska (page 105) as a summertime treat, while Gingerbread (page 107) goes well with winter menus. Because Sand Tarts (page 110) seemed too fancy for the cookie chapter, they ended up in desserts—it's a simple dessert, to be sure, but a nice ending to almost any meal. The dessert to make for a large gathering is Glorified Rice (page 108). It travels well; make it next time you're asked to bring dessert to a potluck supper.

Baked Alaska in a Flowerpot

·Baked Alaska in a Flowerpot·

Traditionally, Baked Alaska is made by covering a sheet cake with a half-gallon of ice cream and meringue, then baking the cake briefly in a hot oven. The meringue acts as an insulator, which keeps the ice cream from melting. This is a great dessert, but there must be enough people at the meal to eat the whole thing, since it doesn't keep. My variation can be made for as few as two or as many as you want.

Instead of a whole cake, you make cupcakes and freeze them until needed. And instead of baking the concoction on a board, you use terra-cotta flowerpots, available at any hardware or garden supply store.

You can put the whole thing together ahead of time and just pop it into the oven while clearing the table, so this dessert falls into the easy-to-make category. At serving time it makes an impression.

Cake recipe (pages 139, 141, or 142)
   or cake mix

Meringue (enough for 4 or 5 serv-
   ings; can be doubled or tripled
   to fit your needs)
2 egg whites, at room temperature
¼ teaspoon cream of tartar

3 tablespoons sugar
½ teaspoon vanilla extract

3-inch terra-cotta flowerpots, rinsed
Ice cream as desired (about ½ cup
   per serving)
Small fresh or artificial flowers
   (1 per serving)

continued

Follow the directions for your cake recipe, baking it in cupcake tins. Remove cakes from tins, cool, and freeze until needed. (If using the same day, don't freeze.)

To make the meringue, beat the egg whites until frothy. Add the cream of tartar and beat until whites are stiff enough to form soft peaks that tilt slightly. Avoid overbeating. Very, very gradually—about a teaspoon at a time—beat in the sugar, and then the vanilla.

Into each flowerpot, place a cupcake. Add about 1/2 cup ice cream. Top with meringue, being sure to cover all the ice cream. Finally, seal with meringue along the edge of the flowerpot. This step is critical! If you do not seal the edge of the pot with meringue, heat can get to the ice cream and it will ooze out. Put on a baking sheet and then into the freezer until you are ready to pop them into the oven.

Fifteen minutes before serving time, preheat the oven to 425°F. Have the flower decorations handy. Four minutes before serving time, put the flowerpots (still on the baking sheet) into the oven and bake just to brown the meringue. Remove the pots to saucers (or terra-cotta drain dishes, if you prefer) and place on a serving tray. Arrange a flower in the middle of each to look as if it's growing there. Be sure to make some mention of having just taken this dessert out of the oven. It's wonderful to watch your guests' faces when they reach the ice cream, which is still solid.

NOTE: An ice cream with nuts makes a good contrast to the smoothness of the other ingredients.

• Gingerbread •

Makes 16 pieces approximately 2³/₄ inches square

Gingerbread is perfectly acceptable served plain, but it's better served with a dollop of whipped cream and best topped with warmed applesauce *and* a dollop of whipped cream.

1 cup (2 sticks) margarine	2 heaping teaspoons ground ginger
½ cup cider	1 heaping teaspoon ground
1 cup molasses	cinnamon
4 eggs, beaten	½ teaspoon ground cloves
2 cups firmly packed brown sugar	1 teaspoon baking soda
4 cups whole wheat flour mix	¼ teaspoon salt
(page 12)	

Preheat the oven to 350F. Grease a 13 x 9 x 2-inch cake pan.

Heat the margarine and cider together until the margarine is melted. Add the molasses and set aside.

Beat the eggs and brown sugar together. Mix the dry ingredients and add them alternately with the margarine-molasses mixture to the eggs and brown sugar and beat well. Pour the batter into the greased pan and distribute evenly. Bake about 50 minutes, or until a toothpick inserted in the middle comes out clean.

Cut the gingerbread into squares right in the pan, place each piece on a dessert plate, and add a topping, if desired.

• Glorified Rice with Butterscotch Sauce •

Makes 12 to 15 servings

This is a dessert to serve when you want to make a *real* impression. It's the dessert you've been saving those very fancy dishes for.

You'll need a double boiler to keep the milk from boiling while allowing the rice to cook. If you don't have one, put the rice and milk in a medium saucepan and put this pan into a large pan partly filled with boiling water.

You'll want to serve the butterscotch sauce often—on ice cream, over sponge cake—the list never ends.

Pour the rice and salt into the boiling water, reduce the heat, and boil gently for 20 minutes. Drain any remaining water.

¼ cup long-grain white rice
½ teaspoon salt
2½ cups boiling water
2 cups milk

1 tablespoon unflavored gelatin
¼ cup cold water
½ cup granulated sugar

Butterscotch Sauce
1 cup granulated sugar
½ cup brown sugar
⅓ cup corn syrup
⅓ cup butter (not margarine)

½ cup heavy cream or milk
1 teaspoon vanilla extract

1 cup heavy cream
1 teaspoon vanilla extract

Combine the rice and milk in the top of a double boiler. Place it over boiling water and cook until the rice is tender, about 45 minutes.

Soak the gelatin in the cold water, then add to the milk and rice, stir in the granulated sugar, and stir it around. Empty the rice mixture into a bowl and let stand until cold.

To make the butterscotch sauce, combine all ingredients except the vanilla in a small saucepan. Cook over low to medium heat, stirring constantly until the soft ball stage is reached (240°F.). If you've never done it before and do not have a candy thermometer, here's how to determine when the soft ball stage has been reached: Drop about ¼ teaspoon of the sauce into a saucer of ice water; with your finger, attempt to bring it together into a soft ball. If you succeed, the stage has been reached. If you fail and the sauce stays spread out, boil it a little longer and test again. Remove the pan from the heat and add the vanilla. Keep warm.

Whip the cream until very stiff and fold it into the cold rice mixture. Fold in the vanilla. Serve with warm sauce.

• Sand Tarts •

Makes about 12 tarts

Tart Pastry

½ cup vegetable shortening

1½ cups unbleached all-purpose
   flour

½ teaspoon salt

4 to 5 tablespoons ice water

Tart Filling

1 egg, well beaten

1 cup brown sugar

1 teaspoon vanilla extract

1 teaspoon vinegar

Pinch of baking soda

To make the pastry, cut the shortening into the flour and salt with a pastry blender until the mixture resembles a combination of cornmeal and small peas. Add 4 tablespoons ice water. With a fork, bring the mixture together. Use up to 1 tablespoon more water to make the dough hold together in a firm, but not moist, ball.

Roll out the dough on a floured board or between 2 pieces of waxed paper to a thickness of ⅛ inch. With a 3-inch cookie cutter, cut the dough into 12 rounds and use them to line 12 cupcake tins.

Preheat the oven to 425°F.

Put all the filling ingredients into a bowl and mix well. Spoon about ½ inch of filling into each shell and bake 20 minutes. Remove the tarts while they're still hot, using great care since they are fragile—and very hot.

Breads That Pass for Dessert: Quick Breads

When you don't feel like making a cake but know you need something for dessert or snacking, any of the quick breads in this chapter will fit the bill. Each recipe has some fruit or vegetable in it, so it will stay fresh for at least several days. The last couple of slices can always be toasted if they've dried out.

With the exception of the Orange Bread, each recipe is so quick and easy to make that it can be effortlessly converted into muffins. It takes between six and eight cups of batter to fill a loaf pan, so one loaf will make approximately twelve muffins. Plan on baking muffins at a higher temperature (375° to 400°F.) for half an hour. Keep your eye on them, and make a notation of the baking time in the margin of each recipe. (You have my permission to write in this book. In fact, you are urged to do so.)

112 • Mary-Jo Hewitt

Conversely, you can make quick breads from any of the muffin recipes (page 19) by reversing this procedure. All of the recipes make twenty-four muffins, which means two loaves from each. Most loaves take at least an hour to bake at a slightly lower oven temperature, 350°F. A toothpick inserted in the middle will come out clean when the loaves are done.

· Banana Bran Bread ·

Makes 1 loaf

This bread is moist and tasty, and the addition of whole wheat and oat bran makes it healthful, too. Since it calls for just one large banana, I bake this bread on a day when I have that special, very ripe banana on hand, begging to be baked into bread. The result is always one happy loaf.

1 cup whole wheat flour
1¼ cups unbleached all-purpose
     flour
1 tablespoon baking powder
1 teaspoon salt
½ cup (1 stick) margarine

½ cup maple syrup or honey
2 eggs
1 large, very ripe banana, mashed
1 cup oat bran
½ cup milk

Preheat the oven to 350°F., and grease a 9 x 5 x 3-inch loaf pan.
Sift together and set aside the flours, baking powder, and salt.
In a mixing bowl, beat together until fluffy the margarine, syrup, or honey, and the eggs. Stir the banana and oat bran into the egg mixture, then alternately beat in the milk and the flour mixture.
Spoon the batter into the prepared pan and bake for about 1 hour or until a toothpick inserted in the middle comes out clean. Cool in pans 15 minutes before removing to racks to continue cooling.

• Banana Bread •

Makes 2 loaves

Are you looking to use up a bunch of ripe bananas? This recipe will take care of them. If you don't have quite enough mashed banana, finish filling your measure with applesauce or halve the recipe.

This bread freezes very well.

3⅓ cups unbleached all-purpose flour
4 teaspoons baking powder
½ teaspoon baking soda
1 teaspoon salt
2 cups walnut pieces

1⅓ cups sugar
⅔ cup corn oil
4 eggs, beaten
2 teaspoons vanilla extract
2 cups mashed banana
(5 to 6 medium bananas)

Preheat the oven to 350°F. and grease two 9 x 5 x 3-inch loaf pans.

Sift the flour, baking powder, baking soda, and salt into a bowl, add the nuts and set aside.

In a large mixing bowl, briefly beat the sugar, oil, eggs, and vanilla. Add the flour mixture alternately with the mashed bananas and mix thoroughly.

Spoon the batter into the prepared pans and bake about 1 hour or until a toothpick inserted in the middle comes out clean. Cool the loaves in their pans 15 minutes before turning out onto racks.

• Blueberry Nut Bread •

Makes 2 loaves

It will take two large oranges to get the 1½ cups of juice and 4 tablespoons of zest called for in this recipe. Fresh juice and fresh zest *do* make a difference.

2 cups whole wheat flour
2 cups unbleached all-purpose flour
½ teaspoon salt
1 tablespoon baking powder
1 teaspoon baking soda
2 eggs

1½ cups honey
4 tablespoons corn oil
1½ cups orange juice
4 tablespoons orange zest
2 cups walnut pieces
2½ cups blueberries

Preheat the oven to 350°F. and grease two 9 x 5 x 3-inch loaf pans.

Combine and set aside the flours, salt, baking powder, and baking soda.

Beat the eggs and honey together, then blend in the oil and orange juice. Gradually add the dry ingredients to the egg mixture and beat well. Fold in the orange zest, walnuts, and blueberries.

Spoon the batter into the prepared pans and bake for 1 hour or until a toothpick inserted in the middle comes out clean. Cool the loaves in the pans for 15 minutes before turning out onto racks.

•Cranberry Bread•

Makes 2 loaves

A slathering of cream cheese makes a nice complement to the cranberries in this bread.

5 cups unbleached all-purpose flour	1 cup brown sugar
2 tablespoons baking powder	½ cup corn oil
1 teaspoon baking soda	4 eggs, beaten
1 teaspoon salt	1 cup walnuts
2 cups sour cream	1 cup cranberries
1 cup granulated sugar	Zest and juice of 1 lemon

Preheat the oven to 350°F. and grease two 9 x 5 x 3-inch loaf pans.

Combine and set aside the flour, baking powder, baking soda, and salt.

In a large bowl, blend the sour cream, sugars, oil, and eggs. Stir the flour mixture, nuts, cranberries, lemon juice, and zest into the sour cream mixture and mix well.

Spoon the batter into the prepared pans and bake about 1 hour, or until a toothpick inserted in the middle comes out clean. Cool in pans 15 minutes before turning out onto racks to finish cooling.

• Date-Nut Bread •

Makes 2 loaves

I've experimented with four or five date-nut bread recipes, but I keep coming back to this one. However, don't plan on serving it right out of the oven—it is best baked well in advance of when you want to serve it.

3 cups chopped, pitted dates
  (¾ pound)
1½ cups sugar
¾ cup (1½ sticks) butter or
  margarine
2¼ cups boiling water

3 eggs, well beaten
1 tablespoon baking soda
1½ teaspoons salt
5 cups unbleached all-purpose flour
1½ cups walnut pieces

Put the dates, sugar, and butter or margarine into a large mixing bowl and pour the boiling water over them. Stir everything around a bit and allow to cool to lukewarm. Do not let impatience force you to proceed before the mixture is lukewarm. You will be adding beaten eggs in the next step, and you could conceivably precook them.

While the mixture is cooling, preheat the oven to 350°F. and grease two 9 x 5 x 3-inch loaf pans.

Once the mixture is lukewarm, add the eggs, baking soda, salt, flour, and walnuts and stir it together. Avoid beating the batter.

Spoon the mixture into the prepared pans and bake for approximately 1 hour. Test for doneness with a toothpick inserted in the middle. Let the loaves cool in the pans for a while before turning them out onto racks.

• Orange Bread •

Makes 1 loaf

Very nice toasted for breakfast, and just as enjoyable with a cup of tea in the evening.

Rind of 1 orange, very finely
   chopped
1 cup sugar
1 cup water
1 tablespoon butter
1 egg, beaten

1 cup milk
1 tablespoon salt
1 tablespoon baking powder
3 cups unbleached all-purpose
   flour

Preheat the oven to 350°F. and grease a 9 x 5 x 3-inch loaf pan.

In a small saucepan over high heat, boil the orange rind, sugar, and water until a little of the mixture drizzled off the edge of a spoon is heavy enough to hang down in a very thin strand. Remove the pan of syrup from the stove, add the butter, and allow to cool for about 30 minutes.

Pour the butter-syrup mixture into a large bowl and beat in the egg, milk, salt, baking powder, and 1½ cups of the flour. When well beaten, add the rest of the flour and mix well.

Spoon the mixture into the prepared pan and bake for 1 hour. Allow to cool in the pan for about 10 minutes before turning out onto a rack to cool completely.

• Pumpkin Bread •

Makes 2 loaves

For an interesting variation, omit the allspice and add a cup of chocolate chips. It's very, very good.

3½ cups unbleached all-purpose
   flour
3 cups sugar
2 teaspoons baking soda
1 teaspoon grated nutmeg
2 teaspoons ground cinnamon
2 teaspoons ground allspice

1 teaspoon salt
1 cup raisins
1 cup corn oil
1 can (16-ounce) pumpkin puree
⅔ cup cider
4 eggs, beaten

Preheat the oven to 350°F. Grease two 9 x 5 x 3-inch loaf pans.

Combine the flour, sugar, baking soda, nutmeg, cinnamon, allspice, salt, and raisins in a large bowl. Make a well in the center.

Mix the corn oil, pumpkin, cider, and eggs in a medium bowl, pour them into the well, and mix thoroughly. Divide the batter into the prepared pans and bake 1 hour and 15 minutes or until the loaves begin to come away from the sides of the pans.

Allow the loaves to cool in the pans about 15 minutes before turning out onto racks to finish cooling. Do not cut until completely cooled.

·Rhubarb Bread·

Makes 2 loaves

A tasty springtime treat. You'll enjoy this easy-to-make bread at breakfast, as a dessert, or as an evening snack.

2 cups brown sugar

1 cup granulated sugar

⅔ cup corn oil

4 eggs

2 cups milk

2 teaspoons vanilla extract

3 cups diced, uncooked rhubarb
   (about 1 pound)

5 cups unbleached all-purpose flour

1 tablespoon baking powder

1 teaspoon baking soda

2 teaspoons salt

1 cup walnut pieces

Topping

4 teaspoons margarine, melted

4 tablespoons granulated sugar

Preheat the oven to 350°F. Grease and line with waxed paper two 9 x 5 x 3-inch loaf pans. (The loaves tend to stick to even a well-greased pan, so this step is necessary.)

In a large bowl, mix the sugars, oil, eggs, milk, vanilla, and rhubarb. Add the flour, baking powder, baking soda, and walnuts and mix thoroughly. Spoon the batter into the pans and drizzle 2 teaspoons melted margarine over the tops of each. Sprinkle each loaf with 2 tablespoons granulated sugar. Bake for 1 hour 15 minutes or until a finger pressed lightly on a loaf top leaves no impression. Let cool in pans 15 minutes before removing to racks to cool. Cool completely before cutting.

·Zucchini Bread·

Makes 2 loaves

There are almost as many recipes for zucchini bread as there are for brownies. This one is amazingly simple, and quite good.

2 cups sugar	1 cup raisins
4¾ cups unbleached all-purpose flour	1 cup walnuts
	2½ cups grated zucchini
1 teaspoon salt	2 extra-large eggs
2 teaspoons baking soda	1⅓ cups corn oil
2 teaspoons ground cinnamon	1 teaspoon vanilla extract

Preheat the oven to 350°F. Grease two 9 x 5 x 3-inch loaf pans.

Place the sugar, flour, salt, baking soda, cinnamon, raisins, and walnuts into a large bowl. In a separate bowl, mix the zucchini, eggs, oil, and vanilla. Put the wet mixture into the bowl of dry ingredients and stir until moistened. Spoon the batter into the prepared pans and bake for about 1 hour. Test for doneness with a toothpick inserted in the middle of the loaf. If it comes out clean, the breads are done.

Turn loaves out onto racks to cool before cutting.

Secrets Behind Bars

It never hurts to have a few easy-to-make, easy-to-serve, easy-to-transport dessert recipes in one's repertoire. The ones that follow are my stalwart standards. I've gone to many a meeting, church supper, bake sale, or housewarming with one or more of these quick and easy desserts tucked in the back of my station wagon.

These recipes will also stand you in good stead when you're not quite sure what to make for friends expected on short notice, or for those who drop in unexpectedly. And most of these bars or squares carry well in bag lunches.

But most important, you don't have to worry about being a master baker to make them. The first time you try any one of them, I can almost guarantee you'll be successful.

· Blueberry Coconut Bars ·

Makes 16 two-inch squares

Blueberries and coconut make a pleasing taste and texture combination. That's probably why this is one of my most requested recipes.

2 cups sifted unbleached all-purpose flour	½ cup (1 stick) margarine
¾ cup sugar	2 eggs
1 tablespoon baking powder	¾ cup milk
½ teaspoon salt	2 cups fresh blueberries
	1½ cups shredded coconut

Preheat the oven to 350°F. Grease an 8-inch square pan.

Mix the flour, sugar, baking powder, and salt in a large bowl. With a pastry blender, fork, or 2 knives, cut in the margarine until the mixture resembles coarse crumbs.

Beat the eggs and milk together and stir this mixture into the dry ingredients. The resulting mixture will be lumpy. Fold in the blueberries and coconut and spoon the mixture into the prepared pan.

Bake for 45 to 50 minutes or until cake begins to come away from sides of pan and top is golden brown.

NOTE: If blueberries are not in season, you may use frozen ones. Since frozen berries retain extra moisture, reduce the milk to ½ cup.

·Blueberry Crumb Bars·

Makes 16 two-inch squares

These are definitely not in the finger-food category, so plan on serving these bars at home rather than packing them in a lunch bag or taking them anywhere forks and plates might not be available. These bars taste so good, your palate will forgive their lack of elegance.

2 cups unbleached all-purpose flour
½ cup sugar
1 teaspoon baking powder
¼ teaspoon salt

½ cup (1 stick) margarine
1 egg, beaten
1 can (21 ounces) blueberry pie
   filling

Preheat the oven to 350°F. Grease an 8-inch square pan.

Place the flour, sugar, baking powder, and salt in a large bowl. With a pastry blender or fork, work the margarine into the dry ingredients until thoroughly mixed. Add the beaten egg and blend well.

Spread half this mixture in the bottom of a greased pan. Cover it evenly with the pie filling and top with the rest of the flour-egg mixture.

Bake for about 1 hour or until the top is golden brown. Let it cool in the pan, then cut into 2-inch squares. Store the squares in the pan, covered with plastic wrap.

• Date Bars •

Makes about 20 bars

During the 1940s, when I worked at a convalescent home for children in Boston, this was probably our most requested dessert. The girls never tired of these tasty bars and never realized how nutritious they were.

1 8-ounce package pitted dates
½ cup granulated sugar
1½ cups rolled oats
1½ cups unbleached all-purpose flour

⅔ cup light brown sugar
⅔ cup margarine
Pinch of salt
Scant teaspoon baking soda

Preheat the oven to 375°F. Grease an 8-inch square pan.

Put the dates and granulated sugar in a small saucepan and just barely cover them with water. Boil approximately 15 minutes, until the mixture is thick but still spreadable.

Let cool. (To hasten cooling, place the mixture in a shallow dish, or put the saucepan in a bowl of ice cubes.)

With freshly scrubbed hands, make a crumb mixture of the oats, flour, brown sugar, margarine, salt, and baking soda. Spread two-thirds of the crumb mixture evenly in the pan and pat down well.

Spread evenly with the cooled date mixture, then top with the remaining crumb mixture.

Bake for about 25 minutes or until lightly browned. Let it cool in the pan before cutting into 1½-inch squares. With a spatula, carefully remove the squares from the pan for storage, or store them right in the pan, covered with plastic wrap.

•Pumpkin-Cinnamon Bars•

Makes 4 dozen 2 x 1½-inch bars

If you're really ambitious, you can puree your own pumpkin for these bars. I've done it, but I can't honestly say it improves them one bit. Since we get pumpkin in so many forms every autumn, why not try serving these bars as a nontraditional treat on the Fourth of July (using canned pumpkin, of course).

4 eggs

2 cups brown sugar

1 cup corn oil

1 can (16 ounces) pumpkin puree

2 cups sifted unbleached all-purpose flour

2 teaspoons baking powder

2 teaspoons ground cinnamon

1 teaspoon baking soda

1 teaspoon salt

½ cup raisins

½ cup chopped walnuts

Cream Cheese Frosting (page 148)

continued

Preheat the oven to 350°F. Grease a 15½ x 10½ x 1-inch jelly-roll pan.

In a large bowl, beat together the eggs, brown sugar, oil, and pumpkin. In another bowl, mix the flour, baking powder, cinnamon, baking soda, and salt. Stir into the pumpkin mixture, then stir in the raisins and nuts.

Pour the batter into the greased pan and bake 25 to 30 minutes or until light brown. Cool in the pan and if desired, frost. Cut into bars and serve. Refrigerate any leftovers.

A Few New Cookie Recipes

Recipes for cookies take up more space in my files than any other category. Most have been clipped from magazines and newspapers or copied from other people's cookbooks. The recipes in this chapter, however, are ones that I've come up with on my own over the years (except for Gerald's Ginger Cookies [page 133], which I doubt you'll find anywhere else).

For cookies that are crisp on the bottom but not overdone, you must make a commitment to shiny baking sheets. Scour them regularly, tops and bottoms. It will mean the difference between mediocre (or even *bad* cookies) and truly superior ones.

These recipes each make 2½ dozen. To bake this many cookies on two baking sheets, arrange the cookies about 2½ inches apart in the following pattern:

By placing fifteen cookies on each sheet, you'll have room for all the batter each recipe makes. If you don't have time to bake off both sheets, wrap the leftover dough securely in plastic and store in the refrigerator, if you'll use it within the week, or in the freezer, where it will keep for a month or more.

·Cinnamon-Raisin Cookies·

Makes 2¹/₂ dozen

These cookies are dandy for dunking and they pack well, making them perfect for children at camp or on campus.

3 cups unbleached all-purpose flour
1 teaspoon baking soda
1 teaspoon salt
2 teaspoons ground cinnamon
2 cups, packed, brown sugar

1 cup (2 sticks) margarine
2 eggs
2 teaspoons vanilla extract
1 cup raisins

Preheat the oven to 375°F. Grease 2 cookie sheets.

Mix in a medium bowl the flour, baking soda, salt, and cinnamon. Set aside.

In a large bowl, cream the brown sugar and margarine until fluffy. Add the eggs and vanilla and beat well. Blend in the dry ingredients. Add the raisins and mix well.

Form the dough into walnut-size balls; place them about 2¹/₂ inches apart in a staggered pattern on the cookie sheet. Bake each sheet 12 to 14 minutes. The cookies are done when a lightly pressed finger leaves no imprint.

Place the cookies on racks to cool and store in airtight containers. These cookies freeze well.

• Marinas—A Maple-Cinnamon Cookie •

Makes 2½ dozen

Soon after returning from Russia, still suffering from jet lag, I confused ingredients for two cookie recipes. I named the new creation for my Russian friend, about whom I was thinking when the mistake occurred. Marinas are now my most requested cookie at the farmers' market.

1 cup, packed, brown sugar
1 cup (2 sticks) margarine
1 cup Grade A–dark amber maple
  syrup
2 eggs
3½ cups unbleached all-purpose
  flour

1 teaspoon baking soda
1 teaspoon salt
2 teaspoons ground cinnamon
1 cup raisins

Preheat the oven to 375°F. Grease 2 cookie sheets.

Blend together the brown sugar and margarine in a large bowl. Pour in the maple syrup and eggs and mix very well. Blend in the flour, baking soda, salt, and cinnamon. Add the raisins and mix well.

Form the dough into walnut-size balls, place them about 2½ inches apart in a staggered pattern on the cookie sheet. Bake each sheet 12 to 14 minutes. They are done when a lightly pressed finger leaves no imprint. Cool on racks and store in airtight containers.

·Gerald's Ginger Cookies·

Makes 36 two-inch cookies

When it's too frigid for outdoor chores, Gerald Pease, a well-known local farmer, keeps himself out of trouble making cookies. When asked for the recipe, he rattles it off: "Cuppa molasses, half a cuppa sugar, two-thirds cuppa lard, teaspoon ginger, same for soda, and flour enough to make the dough stiff, so it don't stick to the rolling pin. Cook 'em till they get done, and don't burn 'em." When pressed for oven temperature and baking time, he responds: "Aw, 350 for 10 minutes, or something like that."

Here's Gerald's specialty, *my* way.

⅔ cup margarine
½ cup sugar
1 cup molasses
2¼ cups unbleached all-purpose
flour, plus additional for rolling

1 teaspoon ground ginger
1 teaspoon baking soda

Preheat the oven to 350°F. Grease 2 cookie sheets.

In a medium bowl, cream together the margarine and sugar. Blend in the molasses and add the flour, ginger, and baking soda.

Drop the dough onto a heavily floured board, lightly sprinkle more flour over the dough, and roll it out to a 12-inch square about ¼ inch thick. Cut the dough into 2-inch square cookies, a handy size to keep in a pocket for snacking or sharing.

Arrange the cookies about 1 inch apart on sheets, and bake for 10 minutes. Let them cool on the cookie sheets for several minutes before placing them on racks for complete cooling. Right out of the oven they are very soft, but they harden as they cool. Store in airtight containers.

• Molasses-Spice Cookies •

Makes 2½ dozen

People are often surprised that these cookies are soft, since they taste a lot like ginger snaps. If crisp is not for you, you're going to love these, the heartiest cookies I make.

4 cups unbleached all-purpose
   flour
1 teaspoon baking soda
1 teaspoon salt
2 teaspoons ground cinnamon

1 teaspoon ground ginger
1 cup sugar
1 cup (2 sticks) margarine
2 eggs
1 cup molasses

Preheat the oven to 350°F. Grease 2 cookie sheets.

Mix the flour, baking soda, salt, cinnamon, and ginger in a medium bowl. Set aside.

In a large bowl, cream the sugar and margarine until fluffy. Add the eggs and molasses and beat well. Blend in the dry ingredients.

Form the dough into walnut-size balls, then place them about 2½ inches apart in a staggered pattern on the cookie sheet. Bake each sheet 12 to 14 minutes. The cookies are done when a lightly pressed finger leaves no imprint.

Place the cookies on racks to cool and store in airtight containers. These cookies freeze well.

• Oatmeal Cookies •

Makes 2½ dozen

These oatmeal cookies are a nice alternative to the soft ones most people make. I don't put raisins in them, but feel free to add some (one cup will be plenty). Break up a couple in a small bowl of milk and let it pass for breakfast.

2 cups unbleached all-purpose flour	*2 cups, packed, brown sugar*
1½ teaspoons baking soda	*1 cup (2 sticks) margarine*
1 teaspoon salt	*2 eggs*
3 cups rolled oats	*2 teaspoons vanilla extract*

continued

136 • Mary-Jo Hewitt

Preheat the oven to 375°F. Grease 2 cookie sheets.

Mix the flour, baking soda, salt, and oats in a medium bowl. Set aside.

In a large bowl, cream the brown sugar and margarine until fluffy. Add the eggs and vanilla and beat well. Blend in the dry ingredients.

Form the dough into walnut-size balls, then place them about 2½ inches apart in a staggered pattern on the cookie sheet. Bake each sheet 12 to 14 minutes. The cookies are done when a lightly pressed finger leaves no imprint.

Place the cookies on racks to cool and store in airtight containers. These cookies freeze well.

Let Them Eat Cake

I came to marriage quite proficient at most homemaking skills. I kept a neat house, made my own bread, and knew how to make pies and puddings. But as a bride the thought of baking a cake intimidated me.

Although I made my first cake, a simple one, at a very young age, I don't recall cakes as part of my regular diet, thus I was never exposed to (what I felt sure were) the complicated nuances of cake making. True, Mother made Bûche de Noël (page 153) every Christmas, and again on Washington's birthday. (She told us it was in honor of the cherry tree young George supposedly cut down.) But the basis of that cake is actually a jelly roll.

As a teenager I learned how to make Delicious Birthday Cake (page 142) and for many years it and the Bûche were the only cakes I felt comfortable baking. I tried lots of others over the years, but the ones in this chapter are those I found foolproof.

You'll notice that three of them are chocolate cakes—my husband's favorite—and the two remaining others are coffee cakes. All use all-purpose flour. What makes cake baking worthwhile is that in the end you have an easy-to-serve dessert, a tasty between-meals snack, and for many old-time Vermonters, a fine way to start the day.

·Crazy Chocolate Cake·

Makes one 8-inch square cake

This is a cake that's been around for ages. It tastes delicious and is unbelievably easy to make. For this reason, whenever friends told me about it during my youthful days of baking, I always scorned it as not worthy of my skills. One summer I enjoyed this cake at dinner with my friends Betty and Bert Cole, who summer in Vermont from their home in Florida. Since they rent a condominium, they entertain simply, and this cake is one of Betty's standbys. Age brings more than gray hairs; with a little luck, comes humility. When Betty told me how it was made, I finally decided to give it a try. I think you'll find yourself making it often.

Also here is the recipe for one of the two frostings I make. This recipe also came from Betty Cole, who puts it on her Crazy Chocolate Cake.

1½ cups unbleached all-purpose
   flour
1 cup sugar
1 teaspoon baking soda
½ teaspoon salt
3 tablespoons unsweetened cocoa
   powder

⅓ cup vegetable oil
1 tablespoon vinegar
1 teaspoon vanilla extract
1 cup milk

continued

Chocolate Frosting

1½ cups sifted confectioners' sugar

2 tablespoons unsweetened cocoa
   powder

2 tablespoons butter, melted

¾ chopped walnuts

½ teaspoon vanilla extract

1 to 2 tablespoons heavy cream

Preheat the oven to 350°F. In an ungreased 8-inch square pan, combine the flour, sugar, baking soda, salt, and cocoa. Make 3 wells in these dry ingredients. In one well put the oil, in another the vinegar, and in the third the vanilla. Pour the milk over everything. Mix thoroughly with a fork and bake for 30 minutes. (Do you see now why it's called Crazy Cake?)

While the cake is cooling, prepare the frosting. Combine ingredients in a bowl and "mush it around a little," explains Betty. If that's not explicit enough for you, use a fork to combine the ingredients until they're well blended and a spreadable consistency.

Using the broad side of a kitchen knife, evenly spread the frosting on the cooled cake.

•Cherry Pound Cake•

Makes one 10-inch Bundt cake

This is a large, lovely cake that doesn't need any frosting for enhancement. It's fine company fare, but don't deny your family the pleasure. Make it sometime just for them!

3 cups unbleached all-purpose flour
½ teaspoon baking powder
½ teaspoon baking soda
¾ teaspoon salt
1 cup (2 sticks) butter or margarine
2 cups sugar
4 eggs

1 teaspoon vanilla extract
1 teaspoon lemon extract
1 cup buttermilk or plain yogurt
1 cup walnut pieces
1 cup chopped jarred maraschino
    cherries

Preheat the oven to 350°F. and grease a 10-inch Bundt pan.

Sift together the flour, baking powder, baking soda, and salt. Set aside.

In a large mixing bowl, cream the butter or margarine and sugar. Beat in the eggs and vanilla and lemon extracts. Alternately add the buttermilk or yogurt and dry ingredients, beating after each addition. Fold in the nuts and cherries.

Spoon the batter into the prepared pan and bake for 1 hour and 10 minutes. (If it makes you feel better, test for doneness by inserting a toothpick into the middle and having it come out clean. However, this cake *always* takes 1 hour and 10 minutes to bake in my oven.)

Allow the cake to cool in the pan about 15 minutes. Then invert the pan over a rack, removing the pan and allowing the cake to cool completely upside down. To cut this cake, use a knife that is either long, thin, and very sharp or one with a long, trustworthy, serrated edge.

• Delicious Birthday Cake •

Makes one 8-inch square cake

I made this cake for the first time in 1947—under the very watchful eyes of E. Jean Church, affectionately known as Mumsie to the girls at the convalescent home she ran for young victims of rheumatic fever. After spending several winters there recuperating from what was then a common affliction, I joined her staff. Many of my cooking skills came from this gentle, caring woman, who was always willing to share her expertise. We made this cake whenever a birthday came along.

I never tire of making it, perhaps because of all the fond memories evoked each time I carefully pour in the boiling water and milk mixture and watch what happens to the butter and sugar. For me, there's something about putting together these ingredients that relaxes the body and gives the mind time to wander. I hope that making this cake will have the same effect on you.

Although the original recipe says that almonds, cherries, golden raisins, orange peel, lemon peel, and citron may be added, I never do. Feel like experimenting? Now's the time.

The frosting for this cake is up to you. If you have a favorite, by all means use it. If not, try my Cream Cheese Frosting (page 148) or the Chocolate Frosting (page 140).

1 cup (2 sticks) butter	3 eggs
2 cups sugar	2 teaspoons baking powder
½ cup boiling water mixed with	1/16 teaspoon salt
½ cup milk	¼ teaspoon grated nutmeg
3 cups sifted all-purpose flour	½ teaspoon almond extract

Preheat the oven to 350°F. Grease an 8-inch square pan and dust with flour. (Two 8-inch round pans may be used instead if you prefer a layer cake.)

Cream the butter, then gradually beat in the sugar until the mixture is very smooth and the sugar almost completely dissolved. Ever so gradually, in a thin stream, pour in the boiling water mixture. (If you add this too quickly, the butter and sugar will separate; take your time.) Add 1 cup of flour and 1 egg, and beat the batter well for about 1 minute.

Add a second cup of flour and another egg, and again beat the batter well. Stir the baking powder, salt, and nutmeg into the third cup of flour, then add it, along with the third egg and almond extract, to the batter. Again, beat thoroughly.

Pour the batter into the greased pan and bake for 1 hour, or until a toothpick inserted in the middle of the cake comes out clean. Cool the cake in the pan 10 minutes before placing it on a rack for complete cooling.

•Maple Rum Fruit Cake•

Makes 2 loaves

Even people who don't like fruit cake love this one. The prejudice surrounding fruit cakes usually stems from those hard bits of candied fruit. There are none in this recipe—just dried fruits plumped up beautifully from soaking three days in wine and rum.

This is not, however, an undertaking to be treated lightly. Read the recipe through to be sure you're ready to commit the time, energy, and rather expensive ingredients required. I promise that this fruit cake will not wind up as one of those that goes round the world every Christmas, never being consumed.

½ pound dried prunes

½ pounds dried unsulfured dates

½ pound dried apricots

½ pound dried unsweetened
  pineapple

1 cup white rum

1 cup dry white wine

3 cups unbleached all-purpose flour

2 teaspoons baking powder

1 teaspoon ground cinnamon

½ teaspoon grated nutmeg

1 cup (2 sticks) butter, at room
  temperature

1 cup room temperature Grade
  A–dark amber maple syrup

½ teaspoon almond extract

4 eggs

½ pound (1 cup) slivered almonds

½ pound (1 cup) pecan pieces

Three days ahead of baking day, cut the prunes, dates, and apricots in half. Cut the pineapple circles into eighths. Place the fruit in a large bowl and cover it with the rum and wine. Mix well, cover with plastic wrap, and let the fruits soak for 3 days, stirring once daily.

Baking day directions:

Decide ahead of time what size loaves you intend to make and prepare your pans accordingly. If you choose to make two loaves, 8½ x 4½ x 2½ inches, you will use all the batter in this recipe. Other options are round fruit cakes made in tins you may have on hand, or very small fruit cakes made in ovenproof mugs. Simply greasing the mugs very well is sufficient, but it won't work on tins. Round tins and loaf pans must be greased, lined with paper, and the paper greased. Otherwise you will have trouble removing the cakes after baking and cooling.

Preheat the oven to 300°F. and place a shallow pan of water on the bottom rack. Prepare the pans you will need.

Sift together the flour, baking powder, cinnamon, and nutmeg. Set aside.

Blend the butter and maple syrup in a large mixing bowl. (If the butter and the maple syrup are not at room temperature, they will not blend—they will separate.) Add the almond extract and beat briefly. Add the eggs one at a time, beating briefly after each addition.

Gently stir in the flour mixture, beating until mixed well.

Using a large rubber spatula, fold in the wine-and-rum-soaked fruits along with the almonds and pecans. Be sure that the fruit and nuts are distributed throughout the batter. Spoon the batter into the prepared pans, filling three-fourths full.

The size of your loaves determines the baking time. It takes about 3 hours to bake 2 loaves, mugs take 45 minutes, 1-pound tins bake in about 1 hour. The cakes are done when a toothpick inserted in the middle comes out clean.

About 30 minutes before the large cakes are done, remove the pan of water. For mugs, the water pan comes out after 35 minutes, and for 1-pound tins, take the water pan out after 50 minutes. If you are making the large loaves, keep your eye on them during the last hour of baking. If the loaves are getting too brown, cover them loosely with aluminum foil.

It's best to allow these cakes to cool almost completely in their pans before removing them to racks. They are fragile while still hot, and you've gone to too much trouble to ruin them at this point.

Once thoroughly cooled, wrap the cakes in plastic and store them at least 3 weeks in airtight tins or aluminum foil in your refrigerator. (If temptation wins out, give in and slice one of the cakes a little early. It will taste almost as good as if you had waited.)

• Marilla's Birthday Carrot Cake •

Makes one 10-inch Bundt cake

When my children were growing up, I usually made Delicious Birthday Cake (page 142) for their birthdays. When I made my first birthday cake as a grandmother, tradition went out the window and my vegetarian granddaughter got the first in a series of carrot cakes. I threw out that first recipe, my only attempt ever at a no-sugar, all-natural, *very healthful* cake! I hope Marilla was so young she won't remember how terrible it tasted, or what a heavy texture it had. The following recipe is much better, and I've used it ever since.

And as far as I'm concerned, there is only one proper topping for carrot cake—a traditional, no-frills cream cheese frosting. Easy and quick to make, it's a winner, every time.

continued

2 cups unbleached all-purpose flour

1 teaspoon salt

2 teaspoons ground cinnamon

½ teaspoon grated nutmeg

2 teaspoons baking powder

2 teaspoons baking soda

1½ cups granulated sugar

1¼ cups corn oil

4 eggs

3 cups finely shredded carrots

1 tablespoon finely grated lemon
   rind

¾ cup chopped nuts

½ cup raisins

2 teaspoons vanilla extract

Cream Cheese Frosting

8-ounce package cream cheese

6 tablespoons soft butter (not
   margarine)

1 teaspoon lemon, almond, or
   vanilla extract (each adds its own
   flavor to the finished product)

2 to 2½ cups sifted confectioners'
sugar

Preheat the oven to 350°F. Oil a 10-inch Bundt pan.

Sift together the flour, salt, cinnamon, nutmeg, baking powder, and baking soda. Set aside.

In a large mixing bowl, blend the granulated sugar and oil. Gradually beat in 4 eggs, one at a time, and then beat in the flour mixture. Stir in the carrots, lemon rind, nuts, raisins, and vanilla. Gently pour the batter into the Bundt pan and distribute it evenly around the tube. It wouldn't hurt to tap the pan gently on the stovetop or counter to release any air bubbles that may be lurking in the batter. Sometimes I remember to do this, and sometimes I don't—my mother *never* forgot it.

Bake the cake for about 1 hour, or until a toothpick inserted in the middle comes out clean. Let the pan cool on a rack for 15 minutes before turning the cake out on another rack to cool completely.

Combine the frosting ingredients, starting with just 2 cups of the confectioners' sugar, and beat until the frosting is smooth and creamy. Add more sugar if needed to arrive at proper spreading consistency. Spread on cake and let set.

Depending on how much taste-testing you've done along the way, this recipe makes 2½ to 3 cups of absolutely delightful frosting.

• Old-fashioned Chocolate Cake •

Makes one 10-inch Bundt cake

Frosting is nice on this cake, but it's good unfrosted, too.

3 cups cake flour
2 cups sugar
1 cup unsweetened cocoa powder
1 teaspoon salt
2 teaspoons baking soda
1 cup sour milk or yogurt

1 cup corn oil
2 eggs, beaten
2 teaspoons vanilla extract
1 cup boiling water
Cream Cheese Frosting (optional;
    page 148)

continued

Preheat the oven to 325°F. Grease and flour a 10-inch Bundt pan.

In a large bowl, sift together the flour, sugar, cocoa, salt, and baking soda. Add the milk, oil, eggs, and vanilla and beat for 1 minute. Add 1 cup of boiling water and beat 1 minute more.

Pour the batter into the Bundt pan and distribute it evenly. Bake the cake for 15 minutes, then raise the heat to 350° and bake for about 25 minutes more or until a toothpick inserted in the middle comes out clean.

Let the cake cool for 10 minutes in the pan before removing to a rack to cool. Frost if desired, or serve plain.

• Sour Cream Coffee Cake •

Makes one 10-inch Bundt cake

This recipe, and its many variations, has been around since the early 1950s. It's another recipe to pass up if cholesterol is a problem. Since I cut back on cake baking once I started basketmaking (one has to cut back *somewhere*), I was astonished at how vague many of my directions were and just how many of the fine points of making cakes I'd forgotten. In this recipe, the batter is layered with a mixture of nuts, chocolate, cinnamon, and sugar. The directions in my file recipe never mention this step. When I made it after a thirty-year hiatus, I was left with a small bowl of ingredients and no place to put them. The next cake was *much better*.

2½ cups sugar

⅓ cup chopped walnuts

½ cup semisweet chocolate chips

2 teaspoons ground cinnamon

1 cup (2 sticks) butter

4 eggs

2 teaspoons almond extract

4 cups unbleached all-purpose flour

2 teaspoons baking powder

2 teaspoons baking soda

½ teaspoon salt

1 pint sour cream

Preheat the oven to 350°F. Grease and lightly flour a 10-inch Bundt pan.

Measure into a small bowl ½ cup of the sugar, the walnuts, chocolate chips, and cinnamon. Set aside.

In a large mixing bowl, cream the butter and remaining 2 cups sugar, then add the eggs and almond extract and beat well.

In a separate bowl, mix the flour, baking powder, baking soda, and salt. Add these dry ingredients to the batter alternately with the sour cream, beating well after each addition.

Pour half the batter into the prepared pan and sprinkle half the reserved sugar and nut mixture over it. Add the rest of the batter and sprinkle the remaining sugar-nut mixture on top.

Bake the cake for 1 hour or until a toothpick inserted in the middle comes out clean. Allow the cake to cool in the pan and about 15 minutes before inverting it onto a rack to cool.

•Velvet Chocolate Cake•

Makes 1 medium loaf cake

Except for birthdays, Christmas, and church suppers, the only cakes I whip up for home consumption are chocolate ones. This one is my husband Clayton's favorite. Frosting is delicious on this cake, but it's also fine unfrosted.

½ cup unsweetened cocoa powder
½ cup boiling water
1 cup sugar
1 egg
½ cup corn oil
½ cup milk
1½ cups unbleached, all-purpose
   flour

1 teaspoon baking powder
1 teaspoon baking soda
¼ teaspoon salt
1 tablespoon vanilla extract
Cream Cheese Frosting (optional;
   page 148)

Preheat the oven to 375°F. Grease an 8½ x 4½ x 2½-inch loaf pan and dust with flour.

Combine the cocoa and boiling water in a small bowl and set aside. In a large bowl, cream the sugar and egg. Gently blend in the oil.

In another bowl, combine the flour, baking powder, baking soda, and salt. Stir into the sugar and egg mixture, alternately with the milk.

Stir in the vanilla and cocoa and beat thoroughly. The batter will seem thin, but don't fret. That's the way it's supposed to be. Pour the batter into the prepared pan and bake for approximately 1 hour or until a toothpick inserted in the middle comes out clean.

Cool in the pan 10 minutes before removing to a rack for complete cooling. Frost if desired.

·Bûche de Noël·
(Yule Log)

"Complicated but worth the effort" . . . that's what I have scribbled across the top of my recipe for this traditional French Christmas dessert. But, if there isn't a jelly-roll pan in the house, don't even think about attempting this. This show-off cake requires the proper baking pan; no other pan will produce the same results. The pan will be a worthwhile addition to your collection because it can be used for rectangular pizzas as well as other jelly-roll and bar-cookie recipes.

continued

Preheat the oven to 375°F. Grease a 10½ x 15½ x 1-inch jelly-roll pan. Line it with waxed paper and grease the paper.

Cake

4 eggs, separated
¾ cup granulated sugar
1 teaspoon vanilla extract
¾ teaspoon baking powder
¾ cup sifted unbleached all-purpose flour

½ cup finely chopped walnuts
About 1 cup sifted confectioners' sugar

Frosting

1 cup granulated sugar
½ cup water
3 egg yolks
1½ cups (3 sticks), butter, at room temperature

1 square (1 ounce) semisweet chocolate, melted
1 teaspoon very strong coffee, or ½ teaspoon instant coffee dissolved in ½ teaspoon water

Beat the egg yolks until they are light colored and frothy. This might take as long as 5 minutes with an electric mixer. Gradually beat in the granulated sugar and continue to beat until you have a mixture about the consistency of whipped cream. Add the vanilla and beat 30 seconds or so.

Stir the baking powder into the flour and add this mixture gradually to the egg mixture, beating until the batter is smooth. Whip the egg whites until they are stiff but not dry. With a rubber or silicone spatula, fold them gently into the cake batter along with the finely chopped nuts.

Spread the batter evenly in the prepared pan and bake for about 12 minutes, or until the sides are slightly browned and start to come away from the pan.

While the cake is baking, sprinkle a clean cotton or linen cloth with confectioners' sugar.

As soon as the cake comes from the oven, loosen the edges and invert the pan on the prepared cloth, centering the cake in the middle. Remove the waxed paper. Trim any crisp edges and save them to use as cut-off "branches" for the finished log. While the cake is hot, roll it and the towel together (as one) and place it on a rack to cool.

While the cake is cooling, make the frosting. Dissolve the granulated sugar in the water and boil in a small saucepan until the soft ball stage is reached (240°F.). (If you do not have a candy thermometer, here's how to determine when the soft ball stage has been reached: Drop about ¼ teaspoon of syrup into a saucer of ice water; with your finger, attempt to bring it together into a soft ball. If you succeed, the stage has been reached. If you fail and the syrup stays spread out, boil it a little longer and test again.)

In a small bowl, beat the egg yolks lightly, then continue to beat constantly, while pouring the syrup into the egg yolks in a fine, steady stream. Continue beating until cool. (If you run out of patience at the lukewarm stage and proceed to add the butter as directed in the next step, the butter will melt, and will not blend properly. You want to avoid this.)

When the syrup and egg mixture is cool, add the butter in small portions (about 1 tablespoon at a time). When the butter has been incorporated, add the melted chocolate and the coffee and beat until well blended. The frosting will be very soft and spreadable at this point.

When the cake is cool, carefully unroll the towel and cake, and spread the cake with about half the frosting. Again roll up the cake (this time without the towel), place open edge down on a cake platter, and generously spread the outside with the remainder of the frosting.

With fork, finger, knife, or toothpick, make the frosting resemble the bark on a log. At each end inscribe some growth rings. With the leftover bits of crisp crust, make one or two knobs somewhere on the top, imitating cut-off branches. Frost them in the same manner. Be imaginative; this is the fun part! If you have access to fresh holly or some other evergreen, add a twig or two.

Place your work of art in the refrigerator for at least an hour to allow the frosting to harden. This is a very rich cake; at serving time, use a knife that's sharp enough to cut thin slices.

Yes, You Can Can
(Jams and Pickles)

This chapter is a brief introduction to a complicated subject. If you've never done any canning before, there will be new terms and unfamiliar procedures. For example, before you start any jam, jelly, or pickles, you need to know how to sterilize jars as well as how to give the filled jars a hot water bath. My method is not the only way. You might also want to consult some government pamphlets for basic directions, or the classic reference *Putting Food By*, by Ruth Hertzberg, Beatrice Vaughan, and Janet Green (Stephen Greene Press).

Another way to find out more about preserving is to get in touch with experienced folks in your extended family (not to mention that interesting senior who lives down the road or up the stairs). There's nothing so flattering as to be asked to share expertise. Write a letter.

Make a phone call. Knock on a door. There's a lot of knowledge going to waste out there. Tap into it.

Equipment

If you don't have canning jars, you'll need to buy them. I like standard jelly jars or pint canning jars, with two-part screw-on lids. These jars are available at most hardware stores or supermarkets. Unfortunately, unless you live in a rural area you can find them only in the autumn. (Folks who run country stores understand the vagaries of canning fever and always have a few extra boxes in a back room.) I usually keep enough jars on hand so that when my rhubarb is up in the spring, I'm ready for it. And I certainly don't want to be out of jars in the middle of winter, when the urge strikes to make Lemon Curd (page 162) or Wine Jelly (page 165).

You'll also need a kettle large enough to cover the jars with about two inches of water and a metal or wooden rack for the bottom of the kettle. (Keep your eyes open for jars, canning kettles, and racks at yard sales or flea markets; they're an expensive investment.)

Sterilizing

Wash and rinse the jars well and place them on a rack in a large canning kettle. Cover the jars two inches above the tops with cold water. Bring the water to a boil and keep it boiling for ten minutes. Turn down the heat, and leave the jars immersed in the sterile hot water until you're ready to use them. Although some say it's not necessary to sterilize jars if you intend to give the finished product a hot water bath, I do both, even if it *is* like wearing a belt and suspenders.

While the jars are boiling, place the lids in a small container of hot water. The rings should be somewhere handy, but need not be wet.

With tongs, remove one jar, empty the water, set it on your work surface, and fill it with whatever you've made. With an immaculately clean, wet cloth, wipe the top of the jar, put on the lid, and secure it with a screw-on ring. Place the filled, covered jar back into the hot water. Continue this process until all the jars are full.

Hot Water Bath

Once the filled jars are in the canning kettle, turn the heat to high. Start timing when the water starts to boil again. When the time is up, using tongs, carefully remove the jars to a cloth-covered surface for cooling.

Finishing Touches

During the cooling process you'll hear a series of pings as each jar seals itself. You'll know the jar is sealed when the dome top of the lid dips down a bit in the middle.

After the jars have cooled completely, wipe them clean with a damp cloth, label them attractively, stand back, and take pride in your accomplishment.

·Lemon Curd·

Never did anything that tastes so good have a name that sounds so unappealing. Let me assure you—if you like lemon meringue pie, you'll love Lemon Curd. Use it as you would jam or jelly, as the filling between layers of cake, or in tarts.

Juice of 12 lemons
12 eggs, lightly beaten
2 tablespoons lemon zest

1 cup (2 sticks) butter
  (not margarine)
9 cups (4 pounds) sugar

Wash and sterilize 14 eight-ounce jars.

Combine ingredients in a 6-quart heavy pan. Over medium-high heat, stirring constantly, bring the mixture to a simmer and reduce heat immediately. Over low heat, simmer for 12 to 15 minutes until the mixture thickens and will sheet from a spoon. (Sheeting occurs when 2 drops of the mixture cling to the spoon and almost come together before dropping off.) The mixture thickens more in the jar; do not overcook or the lemon curd will granulate slightly.

Remove the pan from the heat and ladle the lemon curd into the jars, screw on the lids, and process in a hot water bath for 10 minutes.

This delicious spread will keep for up to a year on a pantry shelf, unopened, and for several months in the refrigerator, once opened.

· Rhubarb-Strawberry Jam ·

Makes 7 eight-ounce jars

By the time strawberries are ripe in Vermont, the best rhubarb has gone. If you live where fresh rhubarb and fresh strawberries are available simultaneously, consider yourself blessed. To make this popular jam I freeze rhubarb sauce in $1^{1}/_{2}$-cup portions until the strawberries are ready; or I use frozen strawberries when rhubarb is at its prime; or I use frozen berries *and* frozen rhubarb to whip up a batch for Christmas giving.

1½ cups unsweetened rhubarb sauce   *6½ cups sugar*
  (see Note)   *1 pouch (3 ounces) liquid pectin*
2 cups hulled, crushed strawberries

Wash and sterilize 7 eight-ounce jars.

Combine the rhubarb, strawberries, and sugar in a 6-quart heavy pan. Over high heat, bring mixture to a full rolling boil, one that cannot be stirred down. Add the pectin and stir for 1 minute by the clock.

Take the pan off the stove, ladle the jam into the jars, screw on the lids, and process in a hot water bath for 5 minutes.

NOTE: To make rhubarb sauce, cut 4 or 5 large stalks of rhubarb ($^{3}/_{4}$ pound) into 1-inch slices and cook in $^{1}/_{4}$ cup water for about 5 minutes, until soft.

·Spiced Peach Rhubarb Jam·

Makes 7 eight-ounce jars

Some folks like this jam because it tastes so peachy; others rave about its rhubarb flavor. The spiciness keeps *me* coming back for more.

1½ cups rhubarb sauce (see Note,
　page 163)
2 cups peeled, pitted, and finely
　chopped peaches (about
　8 peaches)

1 teaspoon ground cinnamon
½ teaspoon ground cloves
½ teaspoon ground allspice
6½ cups sugar
1 pouch (3 ounces) liquid pectin

Wash and sterilize 7 eight-ounce jars.

Combine the rhubarb, peaches, spices, and sugar in a 6-quart heavy saucepan. Over high heat, bring the mixture to a full rolling boil, one that cannot be stirred down. Add the pectin and stir for 1 full minute by the clock.

Remove the pan from heat, ladle the jam into the sterilized jars, screw on the lids, and process in a hot water bath for 5 minutes.

·Wine Jelly·

Makes approximately 4 eight-ounce jars

It's hard to believe that something that tastes this good is easy to make. Any flavorful wine can be used, but my preference is Port. When I can find it, I use well aged dandelion wine. It's difficult to come by and when it turns up, I treat it like gold.

Wine jelly is best served on English muffins at brunch, or on crackers as hors d'oeuvres. Keep it away from the kids!

2 cups robust wine   *1 pouch (3 ounces) liquid pectin*
3 cups sugar

Wash and sterilize 4 eight-ounce jars.

Mix the wine and sugar in the top of a double boiler. (If you don't have a double boiler, put the wine and sugar in a medium saucepan and put this pan into a larger pan partly filled with boiling water.)

Stir the mixture occasionally until the sugar is dissolved and the wine is very hot. Remove top of the double boiler from the heat and stir in the pectin.

Pour the jelly into the jars, screw on the lids, and process in a hot water bath for 5 minutes.

• Blueberry Peach Jam •
(Carella's Famous)

Makes 12 eight-ounce jars

Before a career took over her life, my friend Elaine Carella made lots of jam. This recipe, one of her favorites, came from a local farm where she used to pick her own blueberries. Ever since she shared it with me, it's been one of my favorites, too.

There's no added pectin in this jam, so it takes a little longer to make than most. It's so good, though, you won't mind.

1½ quarts (6 cups) blueberries   *1 cup water*
6 cups peeled and pitted peaches   *7¾ cups sugar*
  (1½ pounds)

Wash and sterilize 12 eight-ounce jars.

Chop or grind the fruit until fine. (This can be done by hand, with a manual or automatic food grinder, or in a food processor. If using the latter, add the water now and do it in 2 batches.)

Place the fruit and water in a 6-quart heavy pan, heat the mixture to boiling, and cover it. Reduce the heat to low and cook the fruit for 10 minutes.

Stir in the sugar and cook until it dissolves and the mixture boils. Let it boil hard for approximately 15 minutes, or until the fruit is clear and the jam has reached a spreadable consistency.

Remove the pan from heat, ladle the jam into the jars, screw on the lids, and process in a hot water bath for 5 minutes.

• Orange Marmalade Mumsie's Way •

Makes 5 pints

There are those who insist only Seville oranges may be used for marmalade. I challenge that. Lacking Seville oranges, Jean (Mumsie) Church, a wonderful woman who taught me many kitchen skills, nevertheless made the best marmalade I've tasted. Although the directions I copied from her notebook are scant, even after a forty-year hiatus I can still make marmalade Mumsie's way.

If you're a working person, plan on making marmalade on your days off. It's a three-day process.

1 large navel orange   *1 lemon*
1 thin-skinned grapefruit   *Approximately 12 cups sugar*

Day 1: Peel the fruits, and with an extraordinarily sharp knife, cut them up. Slice the rinds very, very thin and chop the pulp very fine. The thinner you slice the rinds, the more certain you are to eliminate any bitter taste. Discard all seeds and stem ends as you go along.

Carefully measure the rind and pulp into a 6- to 8-quart kettle.

continued

For every cup of fruit, add 3 cups of water. (Depending on the size of the fruits, there will probably be 4 cups of rind and pulp, which means 12 cups of water.) Let it stand overnight.

Day 2: In the morning, bring the mixture to a boil and boil it for 30 minutes. Take the kettle off the heat and let it cool. Cover the top, and put the mixture out of the way until tomorrow.

Day 3: Measure the liquid into a bowl. Write down how much you have so there won't be any mistake. (It should be about 12 cups.) Return the liquid to the kettle and add 1 cup of sugar for every cup of liquid. Place the kettle over high heat and boil for about 1½ hours. Although the boiling starts at high heat, adjust the heat downward as needed to keep the marmalade from boiling over.

Meanwhile, wash and sterilize 5 pint jars.

Near the end of 1½ hours, keep your eye on the mixture. When the hard rolling boil rises up in a foam that is resistant to stirring down, it's time to start testing for doneness.

Remove the marmalade from the heat. Place a little on a cold saucer and put the saucer in the refrigerator for 2 minutes. Draw your finger through it. It will wrinkle if the marmalade is ready. If it's not, return the kettle to the heat for a while longer and retest. When it's ready, ladle the marmalade into the sterilized jars, screw on the lids, and process in a hot water bath for 5 minutes.

Remove the jars from the water and place them on a board or racks to cool. During the first hour of cooling, shake each jar vigorously every 20 minutes, three times. This keeps the fruit from floating and the juice from settling.

•Watermelon Rind Pickles•

Makes 5 eight-ounce jars

Here's another "use it up" recipe. Instead of throwing away the rind from your next watermelon, transform it into sweet and spicy pickles. In the middle of the winter it's fun to think you're still eating last summer's treat.

7 cups watermelon rind, pared of
    pink and skin and cut into
    ½-inch cubes
5 cups water
¼ cup pickling salt
2 cups sugar

1 cup white vinegar
1 tablespoon broken stick cinnamon
½ teaspoon whole cloves
1 teaspoon whole allspice
½ lemon, thinly sliced

    Soak the watermelon rind overnight in a brine of 4 cups water and the salt.

    In the morning, rinse the rind, cover it with cold water, and cook it over low heat (the water should be barely bubbling) until it is tender, about 1 hour. Drain the liquid from the rind.

    Wash and sterilize 5 eight-ounce jars.

    While the jars are boiling, combine the sugar, vinegar, cinnamon, cloves, and allspice with remaining 1 cup of water in a small saucepan. Bring it to a boil, turn down the heat, and let it simmer for 10 minutes.

continued

In a 3- or 4-quart pan, combine the drained rind, sugar and spice syrup, and the lemon. Simmer this mixture until the rind is clear, 15 to 20 minutes.

Spoon the rind and syrup into the sterilized jars, screw on the lids, and process in a hot water bath for 5 minutes.

·Green Tomato Pickles·
(The Sweet Kind)

Makes 7 pints

Because Vermont gets a good long growing season only once every five or six years, many youngsters think it's odd to see red tomatoes growing on the vine. Green tomatoes? We have plenty of them, and just as many uses for them. This recipe uses a peck, which is probably the amount left on three vines before the first killing frost. If twelve plants were put in, that still leaves three pecks of green tomatoes to contend with. (And just how often can you serve them fried?)

1 peck of green tomatoes
9 medium onions, peeled
¾ cup pickling salt
3 cups cider vinegar

2 cups brown sugar
5 cups granulated sugar
2 tablespoons pickling spice

The night before, wash the tomatoes in cool water.

Into a very large kettle, slice the tomatoes about $\frac{1}{8}$ inch thick. When you have a layer of tomatoes 2 inches thick, cover them with 3 thinly sliced onions. Sprinkle about 2 tablespoons of salt over them. Repeat this process twice. Now add a layer of the remaining tomatoes and the remaining salt.

Place a large plate over the slices and weight it with a large pot or bowl full of water. Let it stand overnight.

The next morning, a brine will have formed covering the plate and going half way up the pot or bowl weighting it. Pour the tomatoes and onions into a colander to drain off the brine.

Pour the cider vinegar into the large kettle and add the sugars. Using 4-inch squares of double-layer cheesecloth, make 2 bags of the pickling spice and put them into the vinegar and sugar. Bring the mixture to a boil and add the well-drained onions and tomatoes. Simmer for 1 to $1\frac{1}{2}$ hours, until the tomatoes and onions reach a texture you find acceptable.

Meanwhile, wash 7 pint jars and sterilize them.

Remove the bags of pickling spice. Pack the hot pickles into the hot jars, cap them, and just to be on the safe side, give them a 5-minute hot water bath.

NOTE: Old-time recipes simply say "pack in jars and seal." The hot water bath *ensures* a safe seal.

•Picallili•
(Sweet Green Tomato Relish)

Makes 7 pints

Similar, yet quite different from Green Tomato Pickles (page 170), this relish also uses a full peck of green tomatoes, some onions, vinegar, sugar, and pickling spices, but in different proportions and using an altogether different method.

If you don't have a manual grinder or a grinding attachment for your mixer, prepare yourself for at least an hour of hand chopping. I can remember chopping all those tomatoes and onions in a wooden bowl using a hand chopper with a curved blade. Only the knowledge of how good the relish would taste kept me going.

1 peck green tomatoes	*6 large onions, peeled*
½ cup pickling salt	*5 cups sugar*
2 quarts cider vinegar	*5 tablespoons pickling spice*
1 quart water	*(see Note)*

The night before, wash the tomatoes in cool water and slice them ¼ inch thick. Arrange them in a very large bowl or kettle, sprinkling them with the salt as you go.

The next morning, strain off the brine that has formed and chop the tomato slices into small particles ("particles" is the word my mentor, Mumsie Church, *always* used). The pieces should be no bigger than very small peas.

Pour 1 quart of the vinegar and the water into a large saucepan. Add the tomato particles and bring the mixture to a scald.

In the meantime, chop the onions into tiny particles no larger than the tomatoes.

In a very large kettle, make layers of onion, tomato, and about $3/4$ cup sugar until all the tomato and onion and 4 cups of the sugar are used up.

Using 4-inch squares of double-layer cheesecloth, make 5 bags of pickling spice and put them into 1 quart of vinegar. Add the last cup of sugar and simmer the mixture for 10 minutes. Pour this mixture over the tomato and onion mixture and cook it over a low heat until the onions are transparent. This usually takes $2^1/_2$ to 3 hours, during which time your kitchen will smell wonderful.

Meanwhile, wash 7 pint jars and sterilize them.

Remove the bags of pickling spice. Pack the hot picallili into the hot jars, cap them, and just to be on the safe side, give them a 5-minute hot water bath.

NOTE: Look for boxes or jars of pickling spice in the spice section of your supermarket.

·Rhubarb Relish·

Makes 4 pints

My mother made this relish from green tomatoes, but one spring, feeling very inventive and having a surplus of rhubarb, I decided to do a little experimenting. This is what I came up with. It's good with meat loaf, and my vegetarian friends say it can't be beat to spark up tofuburgers. Try to save a few jars for gifting. Your friends will be impressed.

2 pounds rhubarb
2 large onions
½ cup chopped fresh chives
1 cup pitted dates
1 cup figs
1 cup pitted prunes
2 cups brown sugar

1½ cups cider vinegar
1 cup water
1 teaspoon salt
1 teaspoon mustard seeds
1 teaspoon whole cloves
½ teaspoon ground allspice
½ teaspoon ground cinnamon

Wash and sterilize 4 pint jars and have them ready in hot water.
Cut the rhubarb into 1-inch slices and chop the onions coarsely. Combine these with the chives and set aside.
Slice the dates, figs, and prunes and set aside.
In a large pot, combine the brown sugar, vinegar, water, salt, and

spices and boil for 5 minutes. Add the rhubarb, onions, and chives and simmer, covered, for 45 minutes, stirring now and then.

Add the dates, figs, and prunes and cook for an additional 30 minutes, partially covered. The relish is done when it has thickened to a spreadable consistency.

Spoon the relish into hot jars, screw on the lids, and process in a hot water bath for 10 minutes.

The Shopping Basket

· The Shopping Basket ·

Based on the tote made popular by Dianne Stanton, this one features a filled bottom and a twill diamond design on both sides. The oval opening measures 14 by 8 inches and it's 12 inches high. (Note: Kits are available for this basket. See Mail Order Sources, page 200.)

Tools

tape measure
pencil
clip clothespins
scissors or diagonal cutting pliers

bone awl
needle and thread
container for soaking material

Materials

4 filler spokes 21 inches long of ½-inch flat reed

5 spokes 41 inches long of ¾-inch flat reed

6 spokes 33 inches long of ¾-inch flat reed

11 spokes 33 inches long of ⅜-inch flat reed

Approximately ½ bundle of dyed ¼-inch flat oval reed for weaving

Approximately 3 yards of ⅝-inch Shaker tape for handles

Approximately 8 feet of ⅝-inch flat oval for rims

Approximately 3½ feet sea grass for rim filler

Long length of ¼-inch flat oval for lashing

Preparation: Mark the middle *right* side of one ³/₈- by 33-inch spoke, the middle *right* side of one 41-inch spoke, and the *wrong* side of one 21-inch filler spoke.

The Base: With the 33-inch middle-marked spoke placed vertically on the work surface *right side up* and the middle-marked 41-inch spoke placed horizontally *right side up*, create a cross with the 2 middle marks on top of one another. This marks your center. *Be sure the horizontal spoke is on top of the vertical.*

Have horizontal spokes and fillers touching. Some verticals will touch and some will not. Pay close attention. Weave the middle-marked filler spoke (*wrong side facing up*) to the north of middle, a 33-inch by ³/₈-inch spoke *right side up* to the east, leaving a ³/₈-inch space, a filler spoke *wrong side up* to the south, and the third 33-inch by ³/₈-inch spoke *right side up* to the west, leaving a ³/₈-inch space.

Everything is now locked.

Remembering to have the *right sides facing up*, and leaving a ³/₈-inch space, to the east, weave two ³/₈-inch spokes side by side as if they were one ³/₄-inch spoke. Repeat this one more time.

Repeat this process to the west.

Now weave three 33-inch by ¾-inch spokes to the east and another three to the west.

You now have 17 vertical spokes, 1 horizontal spoke, and 2 filler spokes.

Bend the filler spokes up and tuck the ends under the third spokes from the end on each side, cutting off any portion that extends beyond the third spoke. Weave a long spoke to the north and another to the south, *right sides up*.

Add a filler spoke *wrong side up* to the north and one to the south, tucking under ends as before.

Add one more long spoke to the north and one more to the south, *right sides up*.

The base is now complete and should measure approximately 13 by 5¾ inches. Flip the base over.

Creating the Sides: (With the base flat on your work surface, you will work 2 rows from the inside and a third row from the outside. Then, with the sides bent up, all rows are worked from the outside.)

Bend up and crease the corner spokes where they meet each other. Let them flop down.

With a soaked ¼-inch colored weaver, wrong side facing you, weave around the base, over one, under one.

At the corners, bring up the 2 corner spokes as you weave around them so that they are perpendicular to the base. Hold them in this position until you've woven at least 2 more spokes. When you let go, one corner spoke will stay up and the other will go down.

At the end of each row, overlap 4 spokes. (Throughout the basket, all rows are individual, as opposed to continuous weaving.)

Go to the other long side of the basket.

Weave another row in the same manner. This row will hold up the spoke not held previously.

Flip the base over and be sure that all spokes are flattened out. With the *right side* of the 1/4-inch weaver facing you, weave around the base.

At the corners, hold the corner up from the working surface, but have your spokes pointing downward and close to each other. Keep weaver taut. After this third row of weaving is complete, bend the sides of your basket up, gently, at the edge of the base. *Your main concern at this point is to be sure you splay out the narrow ends of your basket.*

While splaying out the narrow ends of your basket, keep in mind that the side spokes on the long sides of your basket should remain perfectly perpendicular and parallel.

Weave 3 more rows of simple over and under.

The Pattern: All rows start from left, *on alternate sides of basket:*

> *Row 1:* SPOKE 8: Weave O3, then U-O1 until the middle 3 spokes on other long side of basket. Weave O3, then U1-O1 until end of row.
>
> *Row 2:* SPOKE 7: O2-U1-O2, then U1-O1 for 17 spokes, then O2-U1-O2, then U1-O1 for 17 spokes.
>
> *Row 3:* SPOKE 2: O1-U1-O1-U1-O2-U3-O2; now go U1-O1 for 15 spokes, then O2-U3-O2, and then U1-O1 for 11 spokes.

Row 4: SPOKE 3: O1-U1-O2-U2-O1-U2-O2; now go U1-O1 for 13 spokes, then O2-U2-O1-U2-O2, and then U1-O1 for 11 spokes.

Row 5: SPOKE 4: O2-U2-O3-U2-O2; now go U1-O1 for 11 spokes, then O2-U2-O3-U2-O2, and then U1-O1 for 11 spokes.

Row 6: SPOKE 7: O2-U1-O2-U2-O2; now go U1-O1 for 9 spokes, then O2-U2-O2-U1-O2-U2-O2, then U1-O1 for 9 spokes, and then O2-U2.

Row 7: SPOKE 6: O2-U3-O2-U3; now go O1-U1 for 9 spokes, then U3-O2-U3-O2-U3, then O1-U1 for 9 spokes, and then U3.

Row 8: SPOKE 3: O1-U1-O2-U2-O1-U2-O2; now go U1-O1 for 13 spokes, then O2-U2-O1-U2-O2, then U1-O1 for 11 spokes.

Row 9: SPOKE 8: O3-U2-O2; then go U1-O1 for 11 spokes, then O2-U2-O3-U2-O2, and then U1-O1 for 11 spokes, then O2-U2.

Row 10: SPOKE 10: O2-U2-O2; now go U1-O1 for 9 spokes, then O2-U2-O2-U1-O2-U2-O2, then U1-O1 for 9 spokes, and then O2-U2-O2-U1.

Row 11: SPOKE 2: O1-U3-O2-U3-O2-U3, then O1-U1 for 9 spokes, then U3-O2-U3-O2-U3, then O1-U1 for 8 spokes.

Row 12: SPOKE 5: O2-U2-O1-U2-O2; then go U1-O1 for 13 spokes, then O2-U2-O1-U2-O2, then U1-O1 for 13 spokes.

Row 13: SPOKE 4: O2-U2-O3-U2-O2, then go U1-O1 for 11 spokes, then O2-U2-O3-U2-O2, then go U1-O1 for 11 spokes.

Row 14: SPOKE 7: O2-U1-O2-U2-O2, then go U1-O1 for 9 spokes, then O2-U2-O2-U1-O2-U2-O2, then U1-O1 for 9 spokes, then O2-U2.

Row 15: SPOKE 6: O2-U3-O2-U3; then go O1-U1 for 9 spokes, then U3-O2-U3-O2-U3, then go O1-U1 for 9 spokes, then U3.

Row 16: Same as row 14.
Row 17: Same as row 13.
Row 18: Same as row 12.
Row 19: Same as row 11.
Row 20: Same as row 10.
Row 21: Same as row 9.
Row 22: Same as row 8.
Row 23: Same as row 7.
Row 24: Same as row 6.
Row 25: Same as row 5.
Row 26: Same as row 4.
Row 27: Same as row 3.
Row 28: Same as row 2.
Row 29: Same as row 1.

You will now work 5 rows of simple O1-U1.

Cut off the inner spokes flush with the top of the basket. Cut the outer spokes long enough to tuck into at least 2 rows of weaving.

Soak the remaining spoke ends and tuck.

Inserting the Handle: Starting at the bottom, insert the tape under the weavers that are on top of the third spoke in from one corner on a long side. Now backtrack and tuck the tape under the closest base spoke. Allow about 5 inches to "dangle." (You will be attaching both ends of the handle at this point.) Without twisting the tape, insert the long end of the tape under the two weavers closest to the top (not including the last row woven). Leave a length for the handle, and go back down the same side on top of the third spoke from the other corner, under the matching 2 weavers on the other side. Now insert the tape under the matching 2 bottom weavers. Bring the tape under the basket and repeat on side 2 what you did on the first side.

Place the 2 ends of tape on top of one another and sew them together. Hide the sewn portion under a base spoke and adjust the handles until they are equal.

Rims: From the ⅝-inch flat oval, cut 2 pieces the circumference of the basket, plus enough for a 4-inch overlap. Remember that the inner rim should be about 2 inches shorter than the outer rim.

The overlaps should be on the same long side of the basket, beside each other.

After clipping the inner rim to the basket, toss the tape handles inside the basket and clip on the outer rim.

Insert sea grass as a rim filler.

Lashing: Using ¼-inch flat oval, begin lashing just beyond the rim overlaps. This way they are the last parts to be lashed and any slack or tautness is all in the same area and easier to correct. Lash in whatever manner you've found comfortable.

No Place Else to Go

I feel the need to apologize for this catch-all chapter, but the title says it all. Some of the recipes I wanted to share with you had no place else to go.

After my daughter first fed Cinnamon Flop (page 184) to me I've fallen back on it so often I knew it had to be included. But I had no breakfast chapter. Where to put it?

Mincemeat (page 198). Not a dessert until it's put into a pie, and there are no other pie recipes in this book. Where to put it?

The potato salad (page 196) almost ended up with casseroles, but I didn't think I could get by with that. All three children insisted it couldn't be left out. "It's *you*," they hounded. I had to put it somewhere.

Yogurt wound up here.

Tomato aspic? Croutons? Granola? Bouquet garni? They all needed a home, and this is it. There was no place else to go.

·Cinnamon Flop·
(A Breakfast)

Makes 4 servings

Marion Jessell, my son-in-law's *other* grandmother, heard this recipe on the radio many years ago. Considering the ingredients, it must have been broadcast during the Great Depression. It's a breakfast you can make even if your cupboard's almost bare, and that was frequently the case during those lean years.

3 tablespoons margarine, melted
½ cup sugar
1 cup unbleached all-purpose
  flour

½ cup milk, or ½ cup water, mixed
  with 4 tablespoons dry milk
1 teaspoon baking powder
Cinnamon sugar (see Note)

Preheat the oven to 375°F. Lightly grease any size pie plate.

Using your hands or the back of a large spoon, mix 1 tablespoon of the margarine, the sugar, flour, milk, and baking powder. Pat this mixture into the pie plate and sprinkle it as lightly or heavily as you choose with cinnamon sugar. Melt the remaining 2 tablespoons of margarine and drizzle it over what's in the pie plate and bake for 20 minutes.

Slice it like a pie and "flop" it onto waiting plates.

NOTE: Cinnamon sugar is 6 parts sugar to 1 part cinnamon; try 2 tablespoons sugar mixed with 1 teaspoon cinnamon.

Yogurt, the Earth Friendly Way

For Christmas many years ago, my friend Ann Jackson gave me an insulated box covered with dainty wallpaper. In the box was a quart of her homemade yogurt and directions for making it. I think this was her version of "Give a man a fish and he eats for a day; teach him to fish and he eats for a lifetime."

I ate great yogurt for a long time using Ann's method and never deviated from her explicit directions. But there came a stormy weekend when I couldn't shop for the milk I needed to make yogurt the following day. Necessity being the mother of invention, I proceeded to innovate.

The original recipe said to heat milk to the scalding point, then let it cool to tepid (110°F.). I decided to reconstitute dry milk to double strength in water at 110° and go from there. It worked! I've been making yogurt my way ever since.

I know people who make yogurt simply by wrapping their warmed milk and yogurt starter in a couple of wool sweaters, a blanket, or down vest, others who insist that an oven warmed slightly, then turned off, does the trick; while still others rely on an insulated cooler. I've even been told that in very warm climates the warm milk is put into bisque-fired pots and evaporation causes the yogurt to thicken. I like Ann's insulated box because it looks pretty sitting on the counter, and it takes up so little space.

Constructing the Container

You'll need some duct tape and a piece of extruded polystyrene or isocyonate. Don't be put off by those scary-sounding names. It's simply insulating material that's lightweight and easily cut with an ordinary sharp knife. You can find it at any building supply outlet.

Cut four pieces 4½ by 9 inches, and two pieces 4½ inches square. Using the duct tape, attach the four long pieces to form the four sides of a box. Tape one of the squares to the bottom of this "almost box" and you have an insulated container large enough to hold a quart jar. The last square you cut will be tied onto the top during the incubation period.

If you have the time or inclination, you might want to cover your yogurt-making box with leftover wallpaper, fabric, printed shelf liner, or even plain colored construction paper—whatever suits your fancy. If all this seems like more than you had in mind, there's always the wool sweater.

·Homemade Yogurt·

2⅔ cups dry milk   *1 teaspoon starter yogurt (see Note)*
1 quart warm water

Warm a quart jar by running very hot tap water over it. Place the dry milk into the jar and stir in enough warm water to fill it two-thirds full. Stir until mixed well.

I do not use a thermometer for this next part, but if it makes you feel more comfortable, by all means do so. Add enough *hot* water to fill the jar. Stir it 2 or 3 times. Using a candy thermometer, the termperature of the milk should be somewhere between 110° and 105°F. With a clean spoon, put a few drops on your wrist. The milk should feel about right to feed an infant—that is, warm but not hot. If it is too hot, let it cool until the right temperature is reached.

Swiftly pour a little of the warm milk into a cup, add the starter, stir gently, and pour mixture back into the jar of milk. Quickly but gently stir the jar contents. (Speed is important so that the milk doesn't cool down.) Put the lid on the jar, place it in the insulated container, tie on the insulated cover, and place the container where it will not be disturbed for at least 8 hours.

Remove the jar and behold the magic: what was pourable milk 8 hours ago is now thick, coagulated yogurt ready to use as is, or in any of the following ways. Once made, keep the yogurt refrigerated.

NOTE: Buy a small container of plain yogurt with live culture and use 1 teaspoon of it as your starter. Always save some of each yogurt batch to start the next batch.

Uses for Yogurt

- *By adding several tablespoons of ketchup, ½ teaspoon dried dill, and ½ teaspoon tarragon to 1 cup of this yogurt you have a delightful, very low calorie salad dressing.*
- *My granddaughter tells me that at her day-care center, Iva makes a noncooked dessert by combining yogurt, grated carrots, and raisins. The proportions for this dessert as reported by Marilla were a little outrageous: 61 carrots and 98 raisins in 1 cup of yogurt. Use your discretion. Marilla says it's "Yummy, yummy, yummy!"*
- *You can make your own flavored yogurt by combining it with whatever fresh berries are in season and adding a little sugar, honey, or maple syrup (of course).*
- *And speaking of maple syrup, a few tablespoons in a cup of yogurt makes a nice change from milk and sugar on flaked cereal.*
- *Substitute yogurt in any recipe that calls for sour cream. It won't be quite as rich, but it will be a lot more healthful.*

These are just a few suggestions. Whenever a recipe calls for plain yogurt, use what you've made. It will save you a pretty penny and give you a good deal of satisfaction.

· Tomato Aspic ·

Makes 8 servings

Once a year the ladies of the Gary Home for the Aged in Montpelier hold a potluck supper. They decide what they would take if they were still cooking in their own kitchens and I prepare it for them. I had never made Tomato Aspic before our first potluck, but Madge Locke, age ninety-four at this writing, said that was what she *always* made for one of these affairs and gave me her recipe for it. I now make it at least once a month, much to Madge's delight.

This aspic goes especially well with Escalloped Cheese (page 86) or the potato salad on page 196, as well as any number of other dishes.

4 cups V-8 or plain tomato juice
⅓ cup celery leaves
½ cup finely chopped onion
1 bay leaf
2½ tablespoons sugar

2 teaspoons salt
2 envelopes unflavored gelatin
½ cup cold water
2½ tablespoons cider vinegar

Combine the V-8 (which has more flavor than ordinary tomato juice), celery leaves, onion, bay leaf, sugar, and salt in a medium saucepan. Bring to a boil over medium heat, reduce the heat, and simmer for 10 minutes, stirring occasionally. *continued*

Meanwhile, in a 2-quart bowl, dissolve the gelatin in the cold water. Strain the V-8 mixture into the gelatin and stir well. Add the vinegar and pour the mixture into a 1-quart mold or into 8 individual ½-cup ramekins. (For easier removal of the aspic from the mold, spray it with vegetable cooking spray. Immersing the mold just up to its rim briefly [about 30 seconds] in hot water is also effective but risky, since just a few seconds too much can start to melt the aspic.)

Place the aspic in the refrigerator for about 3 hours to set. Once set, place a serving plate on top of the mold, invert it, and with a little luck, your intact aspic will fall out on to the plate. Slice it into 8 portions before putting it on the table and use a pie server to pass it to each plate.

• Croutons •

Makes about 4 cups

Once you've made croutons from your homemade bread, you'll never serve store-bought again. I freeze leftover slices of homemade bread. When I have enough bread and enoughtime they get thawed and I get croutons.

8 slices bread   Garlic or onion salt (optional)
½ cup (1 stick) butter or margarine

Preheat the oven to 350°F. Generously grease a 10½ x 15½ x 1-inch jelly-roll pan with butter or margarine.

Spread each slice of bread with about 1 tablespoon of butter or margarine. If you want the crumbs flavored, sprinkle the bread with garlic or onion salt. Cut the slices into ½-inch cubes (smaller, if you like), and spread them in a single layer on the greased pan.

Bake for about 10 minutes, remove the pan from the oven, and with a metal spatula, flip the cubes. Return the pan to the oven and bake for another 10 minutes or until nicely browned and crisp. Depending on the moistness of the bread, the time will vary. You may want to flip them a second time. I have had some breads take almost 30 minutes to dry out and brown properly, while others are done in 15 minutes. You'll know when they're ready.

Remove the pan from the oven and let the croutons cool completely before storing them in an airtight jar. Because they've been thoroughly dried out, these croutons will last several months.

· Granola ·

Makes about 24 one-cup servings

Granola is a lot like hash or soup. There are a few guidelines, but the final product depends on what you have on hand. This is the granola I aim for, but not always the one I achieve.

12 cups rolled oats
2 cups raw wheat germ
2 cups sesame seeds
1 cup sunflower seeds
1½ cups walnut pieces
1½ cups sliced almonds

¾ cup (1½ sticks) butter or
*   margarine, melted*
¾ cup maple syrup
¾ cup honey
¼ cup orange juice or cider
2 teaspoons almond extract

Preheat the oven to 325°F.

In the largest bowl you own or a large plastic dishpan, using your hands, mix the dry ingredients.

In a quart bowl, using a spoon, stir together the remaining ingredients. Pour over the dry ingredients in the bowl. Using your hands, rub everything together thoroughly. Spread the granola 1 inch thick in shallow pans. Bake for 30 minutes, turning with metal spatula every 10 minutes to brown and crisp evenly. Remove the pans from the oven and let the granola cool. If you like, add cut-up dried fruits or raisins before refrigerating.

•Bouquet Garni•

Surely you remember the old Simon and Garfunkel song "Scarborough Fair." Did you ever wonder why they needed to remember "parsley, sage, rosemary, and thyme"? To make *bouquets garnis*, no doubt. Bouquet Garni adds an elegant finishing touch to soups, stews, sauces, and some roast meats. There are many herb combinations, but I'm partial to the ones you can buy at the Scarborough Fair.

Dried parsley *Dried thyme*
Dried sage *Bay leaves*
Dried rosemary

Cut double layers of cheesecloth into 4-inch squares. On your work surface, lay out squares equal to the number of bouquets you want to make. Near each square, place a 6-inch piece of twine.

Have ready the containers of dried herbs, plus half as many small bay leaves as there are squares of cheesecloth. Break the bay leaves in half.

Into each square place 1 tablespoon of parsley, ½ tablespoon each of sage, rosemary, and thyme, and half a bay leaf. Bring the corners of the cheesecloth together, secure the ball of herbs with the piece of twine, and place the finished bouquets in a tightly covered container.

Several in a fancy tin make a nice thank-you or bread-and-butter gift.

Until the Tide Turns

While writing a recipe for potato salad I am stopped short when I realize not everyone has access to chive blossoms. Oh, well, offer alternatives. After all, when my chives aren't blooming I pick daisies, or clover blossoms. That's it! Anyone can find a patch of clover.

Really? In New York City? In Colorado Springs? In Los Angeles? Then I think about suggesting time out to look for clover in a nearby park. A little time out is good for everyone. But what about the working mother? How can she take time out when there aren't enough hours in the day right now? And how can I be so sure that everyone has a nearby park? It makes me want to forget the whole idea of including the potato salad recipe with its chive blossom garnish.

But then I remember what it was like growing up in inner-city Boston: sharing a bed with my sister, eating off mismatched dishes, and dressing in hand-me-downs. What pulled me through was daydreaming. I fantasized about a room of my own. Pictures in magazines of daintily decorated houses never filled me with envy, only hope. In my mind I kept hearing my mother's favorite phrase: "The tide always turns."

And it did. But when? Probably when I met Clayton, after I moved to Connecticut to take a radio job I got from a broadcasting school I heard about while listening to the radio as I leafed through a magazine, daydreaming about what life would be like when the tide turned.

So maybe it's O.K. to write recipes that call for popping chive blossoms into deviled eggs. Maybe there'll be someone out there, leafing through my book at a local library, with the image of chives growing outside his or her kitchen door to keep that person going until the tide turns.

• Potato Salad and Deviled Eggs •

Makes 8 servings

Growing up in Connecticut, my children loved the part they played preparing for Memorial Day's first picnic of the season. After I'd made the potato salad, mounded it on a bed of lettuce, and arranged the tomatoes, cukes, and deviled eggs, they gave the dish its finishing touch: a chive blossom propped on top of each egg.

Here in Vermont the blooms come closer to Independence Day. Nowadays, it's our Fourth of July picnic that has chive blossoms peeking out from deviled eggs.

Potato Salad

6 medium potatoes
½ tablespoon salt
12 eggs
¾ cup mayonnaise

2 tablespoons lemon juice
1 teaspoon sugar
2 tablespoons chopped fresh chives

Deviled Eggs

1 tablespoon ketchup
1 tablespoon mayonnaise
1 tablespoon sweet pickle relish
½ teaspoon mustard

2 or 3 tomatoes, a cucumber, some
   leaf lettuce and 15 chive blossoms,
   nasturtiums, or violets, for
   garnish

Scrub the potatoes and boil them in salted water until tender, about 30 minutes.

Meanwhile, boil the eggs until hard, about 10 minutes. Cool the eggs out of water. (Leaving the eggs in water causes the yolks to turn black around the edge.)

Peel the potatoes, cut them into ½-inch cubes (larger if you prefer), and place them in a large bowl. Peel the eggs. Set aside 6 of the nicest looking ones for deviling. Dice the other 6. If you have an egg slicer, by all means use it, cutting the eggs in 2 directions. Add the diced eggs to the potatoes, along with the mayonnaise, lemon juice, sugar, and chives. Mix gently, but well. (You don't want to mash the potatoes.)

Slice through the middle of each hard-boiled egg the long way. Scoop out the yolks and put them into a small bowl. Add the ketchup, mayonnaise, relish, and mustard and mix well.

Fill each egg cavity with the yolk mixture, mounding nicely. Arrange the lettuce leaves on a large platter and mound the potato salad in the middle. Alternately place slices or wedges of tomato, cucumber, and deviled egg. Prop a chive blossom or other edible flower in the center of each egg and arrange 3 strategically on top of the salad.

•Old-Fashioned Mincemeat•

Makes 10 pints

I thought about cutting back this recipe to make just five pints, but reconsidered. Since you're doing it, why not do it up big? You'll want a few jars for yourself, a few to give away, and a few to have on hand for those unexpected gift occasions. If you give away mincemeat during the Christmas holidays, you might want to remind the recipient of the mincemeat tradition: "You'll have as many good days in the coming year as the mouthfuls of mincemeat you consume over the holidays."

1½ pounds lean beef
3 cups boiling water
1 pound suet
2 pounds raisins
1 pound dried currants
3 ounces candied citron
3 ounces candied lemon rind
3 ounces candied orange rind
2 pounds light brown sugar
3 pounds apples, pared, cored and
   chopped (10 cups)

1 tablespoon salt
3 cups apple cider
1 cup molasses
1 teaspoon ground allspice
2 teaspoons ground cinnamon
1 teaspoon ground cloves
1 teaspoon mace
¼ cup lemon juice
2 cups brandy (optional)

Cut the beef into 1-inch cubes and cover with boiling water in a 2½-quart saucepan. Simmer, covered, for about 2 hours or until the meat is tender. Drain the meat, reserving 1 cup of stock.

Grind the cooked meat and the suet. This can be done with a hand grinder, or if you're fortunate enough to have one, the grinder attachment of your mixer. Lacking either, get your butcher to grind the suet when you buy it, and then chop the beef very, very fine.

In an 8-quart pot, combine the meat and suet with the raisins, currants, citron, lemon and orange rind, brown sugar, apples, salt, cider, molasses, reserved beef stock, and spices. With a large, sturdy spoon, mix these ingredients well.

Slowly bring the mixture to a boil, stirring frequently. Stirring is very important in order to incorporate the heated bottom mixture with the cooler ingredients on top. Once the mixture is heated through, lower the heat and simmer the mincemeat for about 1½ hours, stirring occasionally.

While the mincemeat is cooking, wash and sterilize 10 pint jars and have them waiting in hot water.

At the end of 1½ hours, remove the mincemeat from heat and stir in the lemon juice and brandy, if using. Pack the mincemeat into the hot sterilized jars and cover with lids. I use a 10-minute hot water bath, just to be on the safe side, although the original recipe says the mincemeat may be stored in a covered crock. It's best to store it in a cool place.

This recipe yields 10 pints, with 1 pint sufficient for a 9-inch pie. If some of the jars will be gifts, I suggest omitting the brandy. You can always add a note suggesting that 2 tablespoons of brandy be mixed into each pint, if desired, just before putting the mincemeat into the pie crust.

·Mail Order Sources·

Basic Basketry Book

The Basket Book by Lyn Siler
Sterling Publishing Co.
2 Park Avenue
New York, N.Y. 10016

Basketry Material

H. H. Perkins, Inc.
10 South Bradley Road
Woodbridge, Connecticut 06525
(800) 462-6660

The Bread Board

Dennis Darrah
RR #3, Box 1575
Montpelier, Vermont 05602

Kits for Baskets in This Book

Val and Geza Darrah
RR #3, Box 1575
Montpelier, Vermont 05602

·Index·

Page numbers in *italics* refer to illustrations.

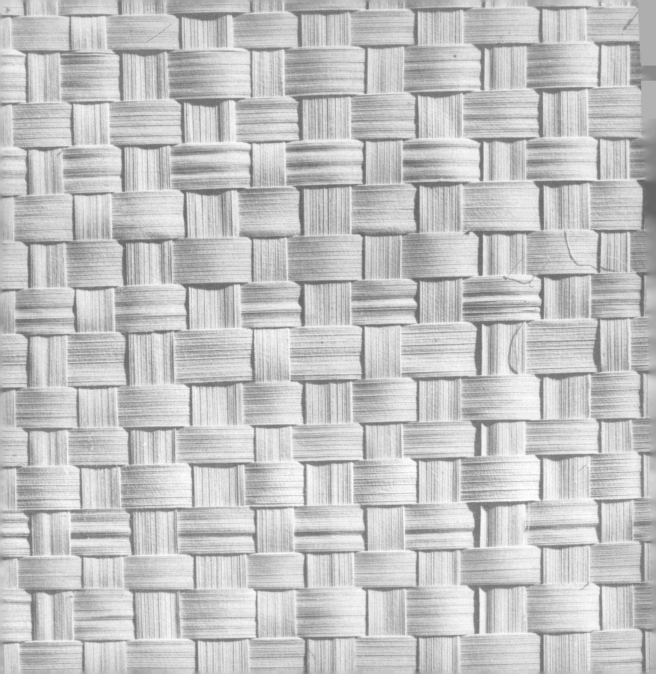